Crown of Blood

A Yoruba adaptation of Macbeth

Oladipo Agboluaje

methuen | drama
LONDON • NEW YORK • OXFORD • NEW DELHI • SYDNEY

METHUEN DRAMA

Bloomsbury Publishing Plc, 50 Bedford Square, London, WC1B 3DP, UK
Bloomsbury Publishing Inc, 1359 Broadway, New York, NY 10018, USA
Bloomsbury Publishing Ireland, 29 Earlsfort Terrace, Dublin 2,
D02 AY28, Ireland

BLOOMSBURY, METHUEN DRAMA and the Methuen
Drama logo are trademarks of Bloomsbury Publishing Plc.

First published in Great Britain 2026

Copyright © Oladipo Agboluaje, 2026

Oladipo Agboluaje has asserted their right under the Copyright, Designs
and Patents Act, 1988, to be identified as Author of this work.

Creative Direction: Shirley Harris

Photography: diva creative

Image Credit: Ryan Hamilton

All rights reserved. No part of this publication may be: i) reproduced or
transmitted in any form, electronic or mechanical, including photocopying,
recording or by means of any information storage or retrieval system without
prior permission in writing from the publishers; or ii) used or reproduced in
any way for the training, development or operation of artificial intelligence (AI)
technologies, including generative AI technologies. The rights holders
expressly reserve this publication from the text and data mining exception as
per Article 4(3) of the Digital Single Market Directive (EU) 2019/790.

Bloomsbury Publishing Plc does not have any control over, or responsibility
for, any third-party websites referred to or in this book. All internet addresses
given in this book were correct at the time of going to press. The author and
publisher regret any inconvenience caused if addresses have changed or sites
have ceased to exist, but can accept no responsibility for any such changes.

No rights in incidental music or songs contained in the work are hereby
granted and performance rights for any performance/presentation
whatsoever must be obtained from the respective copyright owners.

All rights whatsoever in this play are strictly reserved and application
for performance etc. should be made before rehearsals begin to the author
via Bloomsbury Publishing, performance.permissions@bloomsbury.com.
No performance may be given unless a licence has been obtained.

A catalogue record for this book is available from the British Library.

Library of Congress Control Number: 2026930138

ISBN: PB: 978-1-3506-2687-4
ePDF: 978-1-3506-2688-1
eBook: 978-1-3506-2689-8

Series: Modern Plays

Typeset by Mark Heslington Ltd, Scarborough, North Yorkshire
Printed and bound in Great Britain

For product safety related questions contact
productsafety@bloomsbury.com.

To find out more about our authors and books visit
www.bloomsbury.com and sign up for our newsletters.

A Utopia Theatre and Sheffield Theatres co-production

Crown of Blood
By Oladipo Agboluaje

Crown of Blood opened at the Crucible Theatre, Sheffield on Monday 2 February 2026 before transferring to Belgrade Theatre, Coventry from 11 to 14 February 2026.

Crown of Blood was developed with the support of the National Theatre's Generate programme.

CAST

Gboun-Gboun	**Omobolanle Akanbi**
Opaleye/Kundi	**Jude Akuwudike**
Oyebisi	**Kehinde Bankole**
Afilaka/Awosika/Seriki Ogedengbe	**Tunji Falana**
Ayan/Ashabi/Ayebami	**Adeniyi Olusola Morolahun**
Iwalagba	**Patrice Naiambana**
Aderemi	**Deyemi Okanlawon**
Iya Agan/Iyanifa	**Adura Onashile**
Moremi/Ajasoro	**Kayefi Osha**
Arokin	**Toyin Oshinaike**
Ashadele	**Mo Sesay**
Aremo Adekanbi	**Tope Tedela**

COMMUNITY ENSEMBLE

Genifa
Praise Ishola
Antonia Lee
Dami Okhiria
Tayo Olowo-okere

CREATIVE TEAM

Director & Co-Composer	**Mojisola Kareem**
Writer	**Oladipo Agboluaje**
Set & Costume Designer	**Kevin Jenkins**
Lighting Designer	**Alexandra Stafford**
Sound Designer	**Rob Hart**
Co-Composer & Musical Director	**Kayefi Osha**
Movement Director	**Ben Wright**
Fight Director	**Bethan Clark**

PRODUCTION TEAM

Production Manager	**Phil McCandlish**
Company Stage Manager	**Shona Wright**
Deputy Stage Manager	**Olivia Dudley**
Assistant Stage Manager	**Laini Johnson**

Wardrobe Supervisor	**Emma James**
Costumes	**Goldspot Media House, Nigeria**
	Sheffield Theatres Wardrobe Department
Wardrobe Maker	**Sarah Poxton**
Dresser & Wardrobe Maintenance	**Megan Peace**
Sculptor	**Jack Poole, Poile Art**
Scenery Construction	**Belgrade Theatre Scenery, Splinter, Set Blue Scenery**
Production Photographer	**Anthony Robling**
Production Capture	**Pilot Theatre**
Marketing and Communications Consultant	**Shirley Harris, diva creative**
Producer	**Henrietta Duckworth**

UTOPIA THEATRE
Founder, CEO & Artistic Director Mojisola Kareem
Deputy Artistic Director Mo Korede
Participation Manager Bola Akanbi
Reception/Administration Lauren MacDonald

UTOPIA THEATRE ASSOCIATE ARTISTS
Ajide Adeyemi
Lee Affenpinscher
Oladipo Agboluaje
Maria Cassar
Jennifer Farmer
Julius Obende
Juwon Ogungbe

UTOPIA THEATRE BOARD
Maxine Greaves MBE (Chair)
Rhonda Allen
Victoria Barrett
Joanna Graham
Sarafina Manuel (AfroFina)
Bookey Oshin DL
Dr Preeti Raghunath

UTOPIA THEATRE EDUCATION RESOURCES

Discover Utopia Theatre Education Pack for schools and youth groups.

Learn all about the creative processes of designing and directing a large-scale production like *Crown of Blood*, the background of the playwright Oladipo Agboluaje, and take an in-depth look at some of the complex themes portrayed on the stage.

For more details contact *info@utopiatheatre.co.uk*.

www.utopiatheatre.co.uk.

Director's Note – *Crown of Blood*

Crown of Blood is an adaptation of Shakespeare's *Macbeth*, reimagined in nineteenth-century Yorubaland – a world of kingdoms, divinities and ancestral guidance. In this version, ambition, power and moral collapse unfold not on the Scottish moor but within the rich political and spiritual landscape of Yoruba history. By situating the story here, we explore how leadership, prophecy and personal desire collide in a society deeply attuned to fate, morality and the guidance of the ancestors.

The Yoruba worldview amplifies Shakespeare's themes: the weight of moral choice, the consequences of unchecked ambition, and the tension between personal desire and communal responsibility. Yoruba cosmology and spiritual traditions are not decorative elements; they are vital frameworks that shape the characters' decisions, conflicts and destinies. Ritual, music, poetry, dance, chant and oriki are woven into the storytelling, bringing ancestral memory to life on stage and creating a performance that speaks across time and culture.

In bringing this work to the stage, my aim has been to honour both the original text and the vibrancy of Yoruba performance traditions, transforming rather than merely retelling the story. *Crown of Blood* invites audiences to confront universal questions: What do we sacrifice in pursuit of power? How do societies determine who is worthy to lead, and at what cost? The narrative examines the consequences of ambition untempered by empathy, showing how individual choices can shape the fate of an entire community.

This play stands at the intersection of history, myth and the lived experience of the Yoruba people. Though rooted in the past, its themes, the fragility of justice, the lure of power and the moral weight of leadership, remain profoundly relevant today. *Crown of Blood* is a dialogue between worlds, a journey into the human heart and a celebration of Yoruba culture, reminding us that theatre thrives in the shared presence of audience and performer.

Thank you for joining us, for bringing your attention, your imagination and your willingness to reflect. It is through you that this story finds new life.

Mojisola Kareem
Director, *Crown of Blood*
Founder, CEO & Artistic Director, Utopia Theatre

WRITER'S THANKS

To Lekan Balogun

To Ajide Adeyemi, Emmanuel Adetoye, Tobi Bamtefa, Babatunde Euba, Julius Obende, Rose Aida Sall Sao, Olowu Busayo, Theo Ogundipe

To Mervin Claasen, Helena Kablinović, Felix Lier, Yvette Ngum, Eva-Lotte Reimer

To Yvette Hutchison, Oluwatosin Tume

To Sola Adeyemi, Annette Bühler-Dietrich

To the African Theatre Association and the University of Stuttgart

Oladipo Agboluaje

CAST BIOGRAPHIES

OMOBOLANLE AKANBI (*Gboun-Gboun, Spy, Soldier, King's Masquerader*)

Omobolanle Akanbi is a versatile actor, producer, director and consultant with extensive experience across theatre, television and film. He is Outreach and Participation Manager at Utopia Theatre, leading youth and community programmes. Theatre credits include *Death and the King's Horseman*, *Moremi Ajasoro*, *Lion and the Jewel* and *Efunsetan Aniwura*. Television work includes *Jenifa's Diary*, *The Flatmates* and *Jolly Fellows*, while film credits feature *Shanty Town*, *Who's the Boss* and *Omugwo*. Winner of the AMVCA Best Short Film award, Bola's practice celebrates African heritage and champions underrepresented voices through performance, education and community engagement.

JUDE AKUWUDIKE (*Opaleye, Kundi*)

Jude Akuwudike is an acclaimed actor whose work spans theatre, film, television, radio and voice performance. A RADA graduate, he has appeared on Broadway and stages across the UK, Europe and the USA. Theatre credits include *Three Sisters* (National Theatre), *The Convert* (Young Vic), *The Tempest* (Jamie Lloyd) and *House of Ife* (Bush Theatre). Film work includes *Eyimofe*, *Beasts of No Nation* and Disney's *The Little Mermaid*. Television appearances include *The Crown*, *Gangs of London* and *Fortitude*. Jude is celebrated for his versatility, bringing depth and nuance to both classical and contemporary storytelling.

KEHINDE BANKOLE (*Oyebisi*)

Kehinde Bankole is an award-winning actress and producer with an extensive career in theatre, film and television. Born in Lagos, she studied Mass Communication at Olabisi Onabanjo University while exploring modelling and music. Theatre highlights include performances at Shakespeare's Globe, while screen credits span Netflix, Amazon Prime and major Nigerian productions. She made her breakthrough in 2003 on *Super Story* and has since earned AFRIFF and AMVCA awards. Bankole is committed to celebrating African culture through performance, continually exploring diverse roles that reflect heritage, storytelling, and the vibrancy of Nigerian and global narratives.

TUNJI FALANA (*Afilaka, Awosika, Seriki Ogdedenbe*)

Tunji Falana trained at Mountview Academy of Theatre Arts and holds a Postgraduate Diploma in Acting. His theatre work includes *I, Jacques*, *Tom Thumb*, *Reimagining of the Duchess of Malfi* and *How Nigeria Became*. Recent television includes *Suspect: The Shooting of Jean Charles de Menezes*. Tunji is also a creative producer, co-producing *MW: The Musical!* and serving as Associate Producer on Talawa Theatre Company's *Play On!*. His work combines disciplined performance with innovative production, contributing to dynamic, culturally resonant theatre across the UK and Nigeria.

ADENIYI OLUSOLA MOROLAHUN (*Ayan, Ashabi, Ayebami, King's Masquerader*)

Known professionally as Eyinju Olodumare, Adeniyi Olusola Morolahun is an actor, cultural educator and master percussionist. A Tai Solarin University of Education graduate, he is founder of the Abuletic Brand and Kul of Àrt, promoting African performing arts and heritage. Adeniyi integrates acting, storytelling, rhythm and movement in performances and workshops, mastering over thirty-five African drums. Recognised with the Oodua Recognition Award and DAC International Award, he inspires global appreciation of African culture through immersive performance, teaching and collaborations that celebrate identity, community and cultural pride.

PATRICE NAIAMBANA (*Iwalagba*)

Patrice Naiambana trained in African Theatre in Sierra Leone under Dele Charley and Yulisa Amadu Maddy. Theatre credits include *Barbershop Chronicles* (National Theatre), *The Secret Lives of Baba Segi's Wives*, *Tree* (Young Vic), *The Caretaker* (Bristol Old Vic) and *Othello* (RSC). Screen work includes *Criminal Record*, *Death in Paradise*, *Game of Thrones*, *It's a Sin* and *Inside No. 9*. Patrice is lead animateur for Diaspora Performance at The Decolonial Salon. His own works, including *Paul Robeson – Here I Stand*, explore history, identity and activism through theatre, engaging communities in critical cultural dialogue.

DEYEMI OKANLAWON (*Aderemi*)

Deyemi Okanlawon is a Nigerian actor, producer and creative entrepreneur. Since transitioning to Nollywood in 2013, he has become a leading screen talent, starring in films, streaming content and international co-productions. He has headlined multiple Netflix Originals and earned AMAA and AMVCA Best Actor nominations, contributing to hits such as *Omo Ghetto: The Saga*. In 2024, he produced and starred in *All's Fair in Love*, which grossed over ₦130 million. A versatile performer, Deyemi continues to expand globally.

ADURA ONASHILE (*Iya Agan, Iyanifa*)

Adura Onashile trained at Oxford School of Drama and Dartington College of Arts. Her theatre credits include *Medea*, *Creditors*, *Flight*, *Ophelia* and *The Overwhelming* at venues including the National Theatre of Scotland, Lyceum, RSC and Young Vic. She has also performed in site-specific and dance works for The Place, WOMAD and Clod Ensemble. Television credits include *Mayflies*, *Annika* and *River City*, while radio work includes BBC Radio 3 and 4. Adura's work spans classical, contemporary and experimental theatre, focusing on storytelling that blends performance, movement and voice across national and international stages.

KAYEFI OSHA (*Moremi Ajasoro, Woman, Co-Composer, Musical Director*)

Deborah Lawal, known as Kayefi, is an award-winning Nigerian folk and Afro-soul singer, songwriter and creative director based in the UK. Drawing on Yoruba heritage, Ijala chants and African rhythms, she creates culturally rooted and globally resonant music. She has performed across Nigeria, South Africa, Benin, Guinea and the UK, winning awards including Best Traditional Music of Modern Inspiration and Best Female Vocalist (SICA Festival). Kayefi composed original music for theatre, including *Death and the King's Horseman*, and created *Tales and Tunes*, merging music with oral storytelling, championing African culture through sound and performance.

TOYIN OSHINAIKE (*Arokin*)

Toyin Oshinaike is an actor and director with over thirty years of experience on African and international stages. He has played Elesin Oba (*Death and the King's Horseman*), Baroka (*The Lion and the Jewel*) and Obierika (*Things Fall Apart*), among others. Directing credits include *Echoes from the Lagoon*, *Fela: Son of Kuti* and *King Baabu*. Screen credits include *Roti*, *Still Water Runs Deep* and *Nigerian Prince*. Toyin is also a playwright, authoring *Wat's Dis All About* and *Brats & the Maid of the White House*. His career reflects dedication to African theatre and storytelling globally.

MO SESAY (*Ashadele, Servant, Soldier*)

Mo Sesay trained at Webber Douglas Academy of Dramatic Art and has appeared in British films including *Young Soul Rebels* and *Bhaji on the Beach*. Theatre credits include *The Enfield Haunting*, *Coriolanus*, *Caucasian Chalk Circle* and *Under the Black Flag*. Television work includes *Soldier Soldier*, *Dangerfield*, *Murphy's Law*, *Vera* and *Endeavour*. Film credits include *Christmas Karma*, *Who Needs a Heart* and *It's a Wonderful Afterlife*. Mo is also a writer, with a TV script about Dr Barnardo recently optioned, reflecting his contributions to both stage and screen.

TOPE TEDELA (*Aremo Adekanbi*)

Tope Tedela is a Nigerian actor working across film, stage, and television. His stage work includes performances in Ola Rotimi's

Man Talk, Woman Talk and Ahmed Yerima's *The Wives*. On screen, he has taken on lead and supporting roles in film and television projects in Nigeria and internationally, including Netflix's *Baby Farm*, *Blood Sisters*, and *All the Colours of the World Are Between Black and White*.

Tedela has received several accolades for his work, including awards and nominations from the Africa Magic Viewers' Choice Awards (AMVCA), Africa Movie Academy Awards (AMAA), Best of Nollywood (BON) Awards, and the Diversity in Cannes Short Film Showcase. He is an alumnus of Berlinale Talents.

CREATIVE BIOGRAPHIES

OLADIPO AGBOLUAJE – *Writer*

Oladipo Agboluaje is a celebrated playwright, educator and mentor whose work spans African and postcolonial theatre. Recipient of the Alfred Fagon Award, Peggy Ramsay Award and Pearson Award, he has also held fellowships at Freie University and served as a Royal Literary Fund fellow. His plays include *Early Morning*, *Iyale – The First Wife*, and adaptations of *Mother Courage* and *The Hounding of David Oluwale*. A seasoned teacher, he has guided students at Goldsmiths, SOAS and Cambridge, shaping the next generation of theatre-makers. His work blends sharp political insight with lyrical storytelling, exploring identity, heritage and the transformative power of performance.

BETHAN CLARK – *Fight Director*

Bethan Clark is an award-winning fight and intimacy director, certified by the British Academy of Dramatic Combat. She has choreographed productions across the UK, from the RSC's *Cyrano de Bergerac* and *Romeo and Juliet* to West End shows like *Inside No. 9 Stage/Fright*. Her work spans National Theatre productions such as *End* and *The Hot Wing King*, Shakespeare's Globe, Lyric Hammersmith, and regional theatres including Chichester and York. Bethan brings dynamic, safe and visually striking physical storytelling to every production, combining technical precision with emotional authenticity, ensuring that both tension and narrative flourish through movement and staged combat.

ROB HART – *Sound Designer*

Rob Hart is a theatre and film sound designer whose work blends field recordings, modular synthesis and foley artistry. His designs can be heard in productions like *Long Day's Journey into Night*, *Eclipse* and *The Conservatory of Populism*, as well as Utopia Theatre's *Iyalode of Eti* and *Here's What She Said to Me*. In film, he has contributed to over thirty V&A ASMR videos. An experimental musician, Rob also performs solo and collaborates across genres including industrial, ambient and folk. His work explores the immersive power of sound, creating atmosphere, texture and emotional resonance that deepens storytelling in both theatre and film.

KEVIN JENKINS – *Set and Costume Designer*

Kevin Jenkins is a multidisciplinary designer whose work spans theatre, opera and community productions. Trained at the Motley Theatre Design Course and an engineer by background, Kevin brings precision and imagination to every design. Credits include Utopia Theatre productions such as *Death and the King's Horseman*, *Anna Hibiscus' Song* and *All Our Goals*, as well as shows for Sheffield Theatres, National Theatre and regional venues across the UK. Known for his inventive use of space, colour and texture, Kevin crafts environments that enhance narrative, evoke culture and transform performance into fully immersive experiences for audiences.

MOJISOLA KAREEM – *Director, Co-Composer, Artistic Director, Utopia Theatre*

Mojisola Kareem is an award-winning director and founder of Utopia Theatre in Sheffield, celebrated for reimagining classic works through an African lens. Her storytelling champions authentic voices and challenges stereotypes, blending ritual, movement and music in powerful productions. Under her leadership, Utopia Theatre has become a National Portfolio Organisation, launched a thriving Youth Academy and established a Creative Hub supporting African communities and emerging artists. Recent work includes *Death and the King's Horseman*, *Anna Hibiscus' Song* and *All Our Goals*. Mojisola's practice combines cultural heritage, rigorous craft and visionary direction to create theatre that resonates across generations and continents.

KAYEFI OSHA – *Co-Composer and Musical Director*

Kayefi, born Lawal Deborah Olufunmilayo, is an Afro-soul artist and composer blending Yoruba Ijala chants with soul, jazz and reggae. She has released acclaimed works including *Oreske*, *Idowu Ogbo* and the EP *Crazy World*. Kayefi's music has enriched theatre productions such as *Death and the King's Horseman*, and she has performed across Africa and the UK, earning awards and critical acclaim. A captivating performer and creative collaborator, Kayefi continues to explore new sonic landscapes, merging tradition with contemporary artistry. Her work celebrates Nigerian culture while reaching global audiences, with forthcoming projects further expanding her musical vision and influence.

ALEXANDRA STAFFORD – *Lighting Designer*

Alexandra Stafford is a lighting designer whose work illuminates theatre with sensitivity and precision. Credits include Utopia Theatre's *Anna Hibiscus' Song*, *A Matter of Life and Death* (New Vic), and family productions such as *The Snowy Day* and *Murder for Two*. She has designed lighting for tours and venues including Chipping Norton Theatre, Derby Theatre, Queen's Theatre Hornchurch and York Theatre Royal. Known for creating atmosphere and visual storytelling that enhances narrative and performance, Alexandra's designs balance artistry and practicality, engaging audiences through light, shadow and colour to evoke mood, emotion and the world of the play.

BEN WRIGHT – *Movement Director*

Ben Wright is a world-renowned choreographer and movement director, trained at Ballet Rambert. His leadership includes Artistic Co-Director of Candoco Dance Company and Associate Artistic Director of Skånes Dansteater. His choreography spans opera, theatre and dance productions including *A Midsummer Night's Dream* (Opera North), *Twelfth Night* (Donmar Warehouse) and *Macbeth* (Malmö Opera), while movement and intimacy direction credits include *Chariots of Fire* (Sheffield Theatres) and *The Line of Beauty* (Almeida). Ben combines classical training with contemporary sensibility, crafting movement that conveys narrative, character and emotion, enhancing the storytelling power of every stage production he touches

SHEFFIELD THEATRES

Sheffield Theatres is home to four theatres: the Crucible, the Sheffield landmark with a world-famous reputation; the Tanya Moiseiwitsch Playhouse, an intimate, versatile space for getting closer to the action; the gleaming Lyceum, the beautiful proscenium that hosts the best of the UK's touring show; and the Montgomery, a theatre and arts centre with a longstanding history of championing children's creativity.

Sheffield Theatres is the ticket to big names and local heroes, timeless treasures and new voices, and each year welcomes over 400k audience members. With a longstanding reputation for bold new work, many multi-award-winning shows have been made in Sheffield including *Life of Pi* and *Everybody's Talking About Jamie* which have both enjoyed West End and international transfers before returning to the theatres as part of UK tours.

Other recent transfers include the acclaimed *Accidental Death of an Anarchist*, and the sensational Sheffield-set new musical *Standing at the Sky's Edge* which transferred to the National Theatre and the West End in 2024. Jack Holden and Ed Stambollouian's *KENREX* had a sell-out run in the Playhouse in autumn 2024, transferring to Southwark Playhouse Borough in February 2025 and more recently to The Other Palace for Christmas 2025–26.

Committed to investing in the creative leaders of the future, Sheffield Theatres' dedicated talent development hub, The Bank, supports a new cohort of emerging theatre-makers from the region every year.

In January 2025, the Montgomery Theatre and Arts Centre joined the Sheffield Theatres family of venues. A leading arts centre for children, families and community groups in Yorkshire, the Montgomery is also home to many of Sheffield Theatres' participatory strands for children and young people.

sheffieldtheatres.co.uk

UTOPIA THEATRE

About Utopia Theatre

Utopia Theatre is a bold and influential voice in African theatre in the UK, committed to amplifying African stories, voices and experiences through dynamic performance, innovative digital work and community engagement. Founded in 2012 and led by CEO and Artistic Director Mojisola Kareem, the company has grown into a nationally and internationally recognised force in contemporary African performance. As a National Portfolio Organisation funded by Arts Council England, and supported by the BFI, Utopia Theatre has earned a reputation for ambitious productions that inspire, challenge and entertain diverse audiences.

Based at their creative hub in Sheffield, Utopia Theatre celebrates the richness of African and Western performing traditions, while promoting authentic, culturally grounded storytelling. The company has staged and toured acclaimed productions across the UK and internationally, including *Here's What She Said to Me*, *Anna Hibiscus' Song*, Wole Soyinka's *Death and the King's Horseman* (2025) and *Crown of Blood* (2026). These works are known for their emotional depth, cultural resonance and inventive integration of music, movement and ritual.

Central to Utopia Theatre's mission is community-driven engagement that empowers African communities, nurtures emerging artists and inspires the next generation through programmes such as the Youth Academy, Community Ensemble and Inclusive Ageing Project. Utopia Theatre creates pathways for young people, older adults and underrepresented artists to access professional training, mentorship and performance opportunities, fostering a new generation of creative leaders.

Utopia Theatre's landmark *Making Our Own Table* Symposium, 2026 brings together creatives, cultural leaders and academics to forge a Manifesto for the development of African theatre.

'African Theatre Speaks', Utopia Theatre's podcast series, explores the power, legacy and future of African performance. Travelling through the history and heart of African theatre, exploring ritual and revolution, storytelling and performance, the series asks: Who gets to define African theatre and where will its future take us?

Episodes feature Wole Soyinka's *Death and the King's Horseman*, Inua Ellams' *Barbershop Chronicles* and our production of *Crown of Blood*, tracing how African theatre continues to reinvent itself, on the mother continent and in the UK.

By combining artist development, digital innovation and deep engagement with schools and communities, Utopia Theatre continues to energise the cultural landscape, positioning itself as a catalyst for change within the UK and internationally.

www.utopiatheatre.co.uk

Crown of Blood

Characters

Aare Ona Kakanfo *(Field Marshal)*
Aderemi *aka Ajanaku (the Elephant) – head of the Oyo army*
Oyebisi *– his wife, a princess, formerly enslaved by Oyo*
Balogun *(General)*
Ashadele *– a general of the Oyo army, aka Baba Ibeji (Father of Twins)*
Oluawo *(Chief of Diviners)*
Awosika *– an Ifa priest/diviner, head of the priesthood of Oyo*
Kabiyesi *(His Royal Highness)*
Alaafin Iwalagba *– King of the Oyo Empire*
Aremo *(Crown Prince)*
Adekanbi *– Alaafin Iwalagba's son and heir*
Basorun *(Prime Minister)*
Opaleye *– administrative head and leader of the Oyomesi (State Council)*
Iya Agan *– head of the Egungun (masquerade) cult*
Agbaakin Afilaka *– member of the Oyomesi*
Samu Ashabi *– sacrificial minister, member of the Oyomesi*
Arokin *– the court historian*
Ayan *– a drummer and praise-singer*
Kundi *– Oyebisi's henchman*
Ayebami *– a wizard*
Moremi Ajasoro *– historical figure, heroine of the Yoruba*
Seriki Ogedengbe *– historical figure, head of the Ekiti army*
Iyanifa *– a diviner, Awosika's sister*
Esu *– god of the crossroads, chief inspector of sacrifices*
Gboun-Gboun *– the palace messenger*
King's Masquerader/Masquerade
Soldiers, Courtiers, Servants, Citizens, Messenger, Masquerades, Spy

Scene One

Mid-nineteenth-century Oyo, capital of the Oyo Empire in present-day western Nigeria.

Morning, before dawn. Dirge-like music. The stage is covered in smoke. The spirits of **Dead Soldiers** *walk the earth, seeking the path to the ancestral realm. The* **Citizens of Oyo** *cower in fear.*

Arokin, *the court historian, enters.*

Arokin Nineteenth-century Oyo, capital of the Oyo Empire, ten years under the reign of his imperial majesty Kabiyesi[1] Alaafin Iwalagba. Seeking to secede, the Ekiti have united around the legendary Ilesha warrior Ogedengbe. The Fulani have used this opportunity to attack the capital to bring us under their caliphate. A similar attack when Iwalagba's father reigned forced the capital to move to where we stand now.

A **Masquerade** *staggers in and dies – the heavens and earth shudder.* **Arokin** *recoils in horror. The* **Citizens of Oyo** *scream as they flee.*

Arokin Reports from the battlefield say that Oyo blood flows freely, despite the prophecy of Oluawo[2] Awosika, the Chief Diviner, and the efforts of Aare Ona Kakanfo[3] Ogunwolu, the army chief. Alapinni, head of ancestral masquerades, is slain. Even in the spiritual realm, our world is turning upside down.

Arokin *flees.*

The Alaafin's palace. **Kabiyesi Alaafin Iwalagba** *sits on the throne. With him are* **Basorun Opaleye, Agbaakin Afilaka, Samu Ashabi**. *The palace is far from the battlefield, but* **Ashabi** *reacts with fright to every noise.*

---

1 His Royal Highness/Your Highness.
2 Chief Diviner, the head of the diviners known as Babalawo (lit. the father of secrets).
3 Commander in Chief of Armed Forces.

Opaleye Kabiyesi, I fear it is time we flee the city.

Ashabi *jumps up, ready to leave.*

Iwalagba Ifa[4] says we will prevail.

Opaleye I doubt not Ifa's prophecy but your protection is our utmost concern.

Ashabi Kabiyesi, our prime minister offers wise counsel.

Afilaka Ashabi *Abobaku*[5] fears death.

Ashabi Afilaka, it is my privilege to escort our royal father when his time comes to join his ancestors, but only a fool courts an unnecessary demise. Kabiyesi, I implore you to heed Basorun Opaleye's advice.

Iwalagba Is Oyo a trader's basket that moves from market to market?

Opaleye Kabiyesi, you have expanded the empire beyond your father's dreams. If we must move again /

Iwalagba I am not moving.

Opaleye *huffs in resignation. A noise from within the palace.* **Ashabi** *jumps in fright.*

Iya Agan *enters.*

Iwalagba Iya Agan! I commanded you to flee with the royal household.

Iya Agan Kabiyesi, we were past the city border when who did I see among us . . .

Aremo Adekanbi *enters, arrogant and unrepentant.*

Opaleye (*contemptuously*) Aremo[6] Adekanbi, you are the Crown Prince! You are supposed to be here by Kabiyesi's side.

---

4 System of divination, the oracle divinity also known as the arch-divinity Orunmila.
5 One who dies along with the king.
6 Crown Prince.

Adekanbi   How do I succeed my father if the Fulani cut off both our heads?

Opaleye (*cannot believe his ears*)   Did you hear this miscreant?

Adekanbi   Your father is a miscreant.

Opaleye *approaches* **Adekanbi**. **Adekanbi** *flees*. **Opaleye** *snaps his fingers at him*.

Ashabi   Aremo Adekanbi!

Ashabi *goes after* **Adekanbi**.

Iya Agan   Kabiyesi, given my master Alapinni's death, permit me to stay to represent our ancestral masquerades.

Iwalagba   Iya Agan, you are truly a mother to us all.

Iya Agan *kneels before* **Iwalagba**.

Iya Agan   Kabiyesi.

Gboun-Gboun, *the palace messenger, dashes in and prostrates before* **Iwalagba**.

Gboun-Gboun   Kabiyesi! The Fulani are defeated!

Ayan, *the praise-singer, enters beating a victory drumbeat, along with* **Arokin** *who dances as they sing the victory song. The* **Dead Soldiers**, *finally at peace, find their way to the ancestral realm.*

Arokin   Gboun-Gboun! Tell us how we came about our victory.

Gboun-Gboun   Victory or victory! Our forces were about to be overrun by the Fulani cavalry! Aare Ogunwolu ordered the army to maintain their positions but not Balogun[7] Aderemi!

Afilaka   Aderemi disobeyed his field marshal?

---

[7] General.

Gboun-Gboun Disobeyed or disobeyed! He rallied his men and plunged into the enemy, sowing confusion among their ranks! His fellow general Ashadele followed hot on Aderemi's footsteps!

Arokin Aderemi has saved the empire!

Iwalagba Aderemi will replace Ogunwolu as Aare Ona Kakanfo.

Afilaka Kabiyesi, tradition demands /

Opaleye Kabiyesi, I do not mean to question your choice, but we the Oyomesi[8] must be consulted. Ogunwolu has served Oyo with distinction and is a friend to us all.

Arokin Kabiyesi, never has a Kakanfo been ordered to commit ritual suicide after victory in battle.

Afilaka Kabiyesi, Aderemi is rash. He is the son of a blacksmith. Ashadele is of warrior lineage.

Iwalagba Lineage did not save my empire and secure the reign of my house. It did not remove shame from my bloodline.

Afilaka But tradition demands /

Iwalagba I have spoken. Aderemi is Commander-in-Chief of Oyo's army.

Afilaka *remonstrates with* **Opaleye** *to press their case.*

Ayan (*praise chant*) Kabiyesi, *Iku Baba Yeye! Alase Ikeji Orisa!*[9]

Iwalagba Gboun-Gboun.

Gboun-Gboun *prostrates before* **Iwalagba**.

Gboun-Gboun Kabiyesi!

Iwalagba Send Ogunwolu an empty calabash.[10] When he has fulfilled his final duty, find Balogun Aderemi and tell him to report to us.

---

8 The state council of chiefs.
9 Your Highness, Second to the Gods.
10 Sending someone an empty calabash is an order to commit suicide.

Gboun-Gboun Kabiyesi!

Gboun-Gboun *exits.*

Iwalagba Arokin.

Arokin I will record the exploits of Ogunwolu for posterity.

Iwalagba May you always record the truth . . . (*Softly.*) Basorun Opaleye . . .

Opaleye (*resigned*) It is well, Kabiyesi.

Ayan *beats his drum. They exit singing and dancing.*

Scene Two

The Oyo war camp. The air is thick with smoke and the cries of wounded soldiers. **Ashadele** *watches* **Ogunwolu** *ride away on his horse at a furious pace.* **Aderemi** *enters.*

Aderemi Aare Ogunwolu!

Ashadele Balogun Aderemi!

Aderemi Balogun Ashadele! Baba Ibeji! Where is Aare Ogunwolu rushing off to?

Ashadele He received a summons from Iwalagba. (*Reacts.*) Ogun, god of war, protect me. See how his horse cuts through this dreaded smoke only for it to envelope him with gleeful vengeance.

Aderemi Let me join your prayers with mine, for I passed by a dog that looked like Basorun Opaleye's dog. It was weeping so bitterly, I fled from its sight.[11]

Ashadele *Eewo!*[12]

Aderemi Perhaps he has gone to consult with Kabiyesi to decide my fate.

---
11 The sight of a dog or cat crying is a bad omen.
12 Taboo.

Ashadele *Hawu*, Aderemi.

Aderemi My grandfather named me Aderemi, The Crown Comforts Me, in the hope that I would bend the destiny of our lineage towards greatness. Can one's destiny bend that far?

Ashadele How many battles have we fought where your courage was the best part of our strategy? On those occasions, did Ogunwolu not sing your praise so highly Ogun himself grew jealous?

Aderemi I disobeyed his direct command.

Ashadele Because of you he lives to fight again. Aderemi, I laugh when I see you fretting like a child.

Aderemi Your words have calmed my raging mind. Ah, I shall be glad to hold your twin babies in my arms again.

Ashadele That day soon comes when the gods will do me the honour of reciprocating.

Aderemi *Ase*!

Ashadele The Osun[13] priestess my wife recommended; how did she fare?

Aderemi I wish I could say her potions worked . . .

Ashadele Give it time . . . Your love for Oyebisi will not diminish if you take another wife.

Aderemi Ashadele /

Ashadele Or a concubine.

Aderemi I would be in constant fear of what Oyebisi would do to the child of another woman living in my house.

Ashadele *Hawu*, Aderemi. She would never harm a child, not a child of your blood.

---

13 Goddess of River Osun in Osogbo, Western Nigeria, wife of Sango, god of thunder and fourth Alaafin. She is the orisa of fertility.

Aderemi Can one really know what a person can do when a situation presents itself?

Oyebisi *enters.*

Oyebisi My lord!

Aderemi *Orisa mi!*[14]

Oyebisi *runs into* **Aderemi**'*s arms. She kneels before him.*

Oyebisi Joy overwhelms me to see you alive and unharmed.

Aderemi My love, it was the thought of returning to you that kept my sword thirsty until the last of our enemy was struck down.

Oyebisi Do not doubt that I leant my power to your arm.

Ashadele I take my leave.

Aderemi Ashadele.

Ashadele *exits.*

Aderemi Why risk coming to the battlefield so soon?

Oyebisi Ayebami saw that the war was over and that the Fulani had fled.

Aderemi Where is Kundi?

Oyebisi I bid him stay when I saw you in the distance.

Aderemi I employ him to protect you.

Oyebisi I had a dream concerning you.

Aderemi A dream.

Oyebisi A crown was placed upon your head.

Aderemi And?

Oyebisi Where the dream begins is also where it ends.

---

14 My orisa: a term of endearment.

Aderemi Can Ayebami not crack its meaning, or is deciphering dreams beyond his wizardry?

Oyebisi The Chief Diviner's shrine is nearby.

Aderemi I await Ogunwolu's orders.

Oyebisi A consultation takes no time. Please, my lord.

Aderemi . . . To please you, *orisa mi*.

Aderemi *and* **Oyebisi** *exit.*

Esu, *deity of the uncertainty principle and inspector of sacrifices, stands like a carving. He is dressed in his colours of red and black and a long cap.* **Awosika** *enters with a sacrifice in a calabash and lays it at* **Esu**'s *feet.*

Awosika Esu Elegbara, the most feared of deities, the gateway between Olodumare, deities and humans, who revels in the uncertainty of fate. Forgive me for dishonouring my vocation. Accept my sacrifice and do not obstruct my path to Ifa. Do not toy with me and bend my destiny toward tragedy.

Esu *looks at the sacrifice with disdain.*

Scene Three

By **Awosika**'s *shrine.*

Oyebisi *and* **Aderemi** *enter.*

Aderemi (*to* **Oyebisi**) I won't be long. (*Calls.*) Awosika, it is me, oh.

Awosika Ah, Balogun Aderemi! Please enter.

Aderemi *enters the shrine.*

Aderemi My wife Oyebisi's dream has brought me to disturb you.

Awosika *E ma wo le.*[15] Please sit.

Aderemi *sits beside* **Awosika** *on the mat.* **Awosika** *nervously prepares his divination tools of kola nuts and a string of cowries.*

Aderemi The battle went as you predicted . . . You told me which sacrifices to make and fortified my charms with supplications to Ogun . . .

Awosika *is too preoccupied to respond.*

Aderemi Oluawo, I am alive and well.

Awosika Of course! We are happy that you are alive. May you live long and continue to prosper.

Aderemi *Ase.*

Awosika This dream, what was it about?

Aderemi Oyebisi saw a crown placed upon my head.

Awosika I see . . . Let us see what Ifa says.

Esu *slowly raises his leg over* **Awosika**'s *sacrifice as* **Awosika** *incants and shakes the kola nuts before casting them on the mat. His hands tremble as he shapes the divination beads. He is stunned by what he reads from the beads, as if he cannot believe the reading is true.*

Awosika (*boldly*) Aderemi Ajanaku, son of Ajasa. The Elephant that crushes all who stand in its path. I greet you, Aare Ona Kakanfo . . .

Aderemi Awosika! Did you call me Field Marshal? Ogunwolu still breathes!

Awosika Ifa has spoken, my lord!

Aderemi Your hands trembled. Cast the kola nuts again.

Awosika My lord, these *are* Ifa's words!

Aderemi: Again Awosika! Please . . .

---

15 A greeting.

Awosika *shakes the kola nuts confidently.* **Esu** *steps on the sacrifice.* **Awosika** *senses* **Esu***'s rejection of him. He realises that the link between him and* **Ifa** *is severed. He casts the nuts but gets no reading. He performs the ritual again with the same result.*

Awosika   . . . General! I have a clearer reading of your wife's dream . . . Kings and chiefs shall prostrate before you . . . Second to the Orisas.

Aderemi   Awosika! You replace one heresy with a bigger heresy!

Awosika   It is what I am told to say, my lord.

Aderemi   And Ifa tells you that I, Aderemi, son of Ajasa the blacksmith, will become Alaafin?

Awosika *avoids making eye contact with* **Aderemi**.

Aderemi   How can this be? I am of lowly birth. Iwalagba has named Adekanbi as his successor. I am not a prince of the seven royal houses from which kings are chosen. I am Balogun and Iwalagba's representative of Ilara Town. My hand and willpower have won me these honours but there is only so far they can take me. Awosika, do you mock me?

Awosika   No, my lord.

Aderemi   Does Ifa say how I shall wear the crown?

Awosika   No, my lord.

Aderemi   Awosika.

Awosika   My lord.

Aderemi   Awosika.

Awosika   My lord.

Aderemi   *Awosika.*

Awosika   I am answering you, my lord!

Aderemi *extracts cowries from his pouch to pay* **Awosika**. **Awosika** *presses the money back into* **Aderemi***'s hands.*

Aderemi Ifa's tribute must be paid.

Awosika You are at a crossroads. Sacrifice to Esu to direct your path.

Esu *laughs.* **Awosika** *takes his flywhisk and incants to fortify* **Aderemi**'s *amulets.*

Aderemi Which crossroads is this again?

Awosika I have fortified your amulets. As long as you wear them and they are complete, you will come to no mortal harm. Go well, my lord.

Aderemi *exits the shrine.* **Oyebisi** *goes to him.* **Awosika** *remains in the shrine and faces* **Esu**, *supplicating him, but* **Esu** *is unmoved.*

Oyebisi My lord! What did Ifa say?

Aderemi Something gnawing at Awosika's heart has clouded his vision.

Oyebisi How so, my lord?

Aderemi First, he says I will become Kakanfo. Custom dictates there can only be one Kakanfo at a time.

Gboun-Gboun, *enters, breathless.*

Gboun-Gboun Balogun Aderemi!

Aderemi Gboun-Gboun, catch your breath.

Gboun-Gboun The Alaafin demands your presence at his palace immediately!

Aderemi Why the haste?

Gboun-Gboun Haste or haste! By order of Alaafin Iwalagba and the Oyomesi[16] Ogunwolu was sent an empty calabash!

Aderemi (*shocked*) Ogunwolu my mentor no longer lives?

---

16 State Council.

Gboun-Gboun   His disgraceful action has been erased from memory!

Aderemi   Gboun-Gboun! Mind your tongue!

Gboun-Gboun *prostrates before* **Aderemi**.

Gboun-Gboun   Balogun Aderemi, I meant no disrespect!

Aderemi   Away!

Gboun-Gboun   Yes, my lord!

Gboun-Gboun *exits*.

Aderemi   I thought I was going to be punished, yet it is my master who has breathed his last. What cruel fate is this where the punishment for failure is victory's reward? Ah, Ogunwolu . . .

Oyebisi   My lord, this is no time to mourn. Don't you know what this means? Awosika's prophecy is true. You are to become Aare Ona Kakanfo.

Aderemi   Ogunwolu was like a father to me! It was in his house that I met you.

Oyebisi   You forget I was his war booty, a slave in that very house because Iwalagba wanted to expand his empire. I, a princess, who was betrothed to my homeland's king! He made me watch as he slit the throats of my household. It was his soldier's abuse of me that hollowed out my womb and replaced my blood with bile for Oyo. My household gods! You have answered my supplications for his ignominious end. May his lineage bear his shame until death is their only remedy.

Aderemi   My wife, I did not forget, but please, mind your words.

Oyebisi   Heed the gods! It is your turn now. It is our turn, Aare Ona Kakanfo.

Aderemi   But if this is true, then . . .

Oyebisi Then what, my lord?

Aderemi Awosika said I would become Alaafin.

Oyebisi Ehn? This was Ifa's reading of my dream?

Aderemi One does not expect flight from a chicken nor the chameleon to stride.

Oyebisi Why must you keep disparaging yourself? Ifa is never wrong.

Aderemi Awosika said I must make a sacrifice to the god of the crossroads. This means that the path, like my mind, is clouded with uncertainty. Like your dream, he would not reveal how I shall be crowned . . . I must know!

Aderemi *makes to go back to* **Awosika**'s *shrine.* **Oyebisi** *blocks his path.* **Esu** *turns, holding a bottle.* **Awosika** *thinks* **Esu** *is about to forgive him. Instead,* **Esu** *pours blood over the despoiled sacrifice.* **Awosika** *is terrified as a red stain appears on his robe.* **Esu** *exits.* **Awosika** *frantically tries to clean the blood off his robe.*

Oyebisi He tells you and then what? Keeping this prophecy utmost on your mind will reveal it in your eyes and put our lives at risk.

Aderemi How do I face Kabiyesi?

Oyebisi Accept the rank of Kakanfo like it is the highest office you could hope to attain. Tonight, when we return home to Ilara, we will unpack this prophecy. If uncertainty still clouds your thoughts, return to Awosika. Do not let your rashness that has brought us honour be our undoing. Trust that the gods have willed it. Kabiyesi awaits you.

Aderemi . . . I go, my wife.

Oyebisi My lord.

Aderemi *exits.* **Oyebisi** *beckons to* **Kundi** *who enters from offstage carrying a bag of cowries, which he hands to* **Oyebisi**. **Oyebisi**, *excited, enters* **Awosika**'s *shrine without an invitation while* **Kundi** *guards the entrance.*

Oyebisi Awosika, did Ifa see that Aderemi would become Kakanfo?

Awosika Yes.

Oyebisi Hey! Then Ifa saw he would become Alaafin! (*Dances.*) Indeed, it is not only *orisas* that have the power to bend destiny to our will.

Awosika Ifa said no such thing! I relayed your lie to him as you coerced me to.

Oyebisi Surely Ifa must have . . .

Awosika *shows* **Oyebisi** *the stain.*

Awosika I said I know not what Ifa says in this matter whether or not your lie will become true! Esu has blocked my way to Ifa. I cannot even see my own destiny.

Disappointed, **Oyebisi** *throws the bag at* **Awosika**'s *feet.*

Oyebisi Your conscience was absent when you slept with the queen.[17] Do not let it prick you now.

Oyebisi *makes to leave.*

Awosika My lady, do you not feel the weight of our actions?

Oyebisi You are not the first babalawo to divine under false pretences. If your gods are so powerful you should have been struck down before Aderemi set foot in your shrine. But how would they exist without us to supplicate them?

Awosika Your husband is a good man. He does not deserve to be tricked like this.

Oyebisi Of what use is a good man without ambition?

The sound of drumming.

Awosika You will destroy the empire for the sake of revenge. Your destiny /

---

17 The punishment for sleeping with the Alaafin's wife/wives is death.

Oyebisi I will reclaim my destiny as queen no matter what Ifa says and I will wreak havoc on Oyo for what it has done to me. It is I, Oyebisi, that says so.

The sound of drumming. **Kundi** *sees* **Arokin** *and* **Ayan** *approaching and enters the shrine before he is seen.*

Kundi Arokin.

Oyebisi (*to* **Awosika**)   Do not alert him to our presence.

Arokin *and* **Ayan** *enter with a* **Passerby**. **Ayan** *is drumming the* **Passerby**'s *oriki. The* **Passerby** *gives* **Ayan** *a few cowries.*

Arokin Praise-singing lies for money like a beggar. Where is your honour?

Ayan Will honour feed my family?

Arokin When we return to the palace, we will take the bush path.

Ayan There will be no one to patronise me!

Arokin Ehn, drum for yourself. No one will remember you when you die.

Ayan *glares at* **Arokin**.

Oluawo . . . Oluawo Awosika.

Awosika Oh!

Arokin Kabiyesi sent us. May we enter?

Oyebisi *prods* **Awosika** *to go out and meet them.* **Awosika** *comes out of the shrine.*

Awosika What is Kabiyesi's message?

Ayan Ah, Oluawo, won't you welcome us with palm wine?

Arokin (*glaring at* **Ayan**)   Kabiyesi requests your presence.

Awosika I shall be right behind you.

Ayan Or a few cowries to buy palm wine.

Arokin (*to* **Ayan**)   Start walking . . .

Awosika   Wait!

Awosika *enters the shrine.* **Kundi** *makes to draw his sword.* **Awosika** *picks up the bag of cowries and gives it to* **Ayan**.

Ayan   Ah! Baba!

Ecstatic, **Ayan** *drums* **Awosika**'s *oriki.*

Ayan (*chants*)   Awosika, Father of Diviners . . .

Awosika   Enough . . .

Ayan   . . . The incorruptible voice of Ifa . . .

Awosika   I said stop!

Ayan *stops.*

Arokin   Oluawo, is everything well with you? Oluawo . . .

Awosika *enters the shrine and gathers his paraphernalia.*

Arokin *and* **Ayan** *head in the direction of* **Awosika**'s *sacrifice to* **Esu**. **Arokin** *notices it.* **Ayan** *is too preoccupied with the money to notice.* **Arokin** *ponders, looking in* **Awosika**'s *direction, then exits after* **Ayan**.

Oyebisi   Aderemi is at the palace.

Awosika *ignores her as he finishes packing up.*

Oyebisi   The stain will tell them you have dishonoured your calling and lead your crime back to me. Awosika. Awosika!

Kundi *blocks* **Awosika**'s *way and draws his sword.*

Awosika   Kundi, please, I have no quarrel with you.

Oyebisi   Kill him!

Kundi *makes to strike* **Awosika**. **Awosika** *casts a spell on him with his amulet.*

Awosika Stand still! The worm and the snake slither. We fear the snake but crush the worm. If I say flesh must turn to stone, then flesh must obey. Stand still!

Oyebisi *brings out a dagger from her wrapper and hovers an amulet over it while* **Kundi** *struggles to strike* **Awosika** . . .

Awosika Kundi, I said stand still!

. . . *but* **Awosika**'s *spell is too strong.* **Kundi** *stands rigid.* **Oyebisi** *stabs* **Awosika**.

Oyebisi Ayebami! You are indeed the king of wizards.

Awosika *dies.* **Oyebisi** *looks at the knife in her hands. She feels faint.*

Oyebisi Do not faint, Oyebisi! You must be strong to guide Aderemi's sword into the heart of Oyo. The blood of your family demands it.

The smoke clears.

The smoke clears. This is a sign! My household gods, rend fear from my heart! Does the iroko tree bend? Be resolute, Oyebisi, be resolute . . .

Oyebisi *wipes the blood from the dagger and her hands on a cloth.*

Oyebisi Dump his body in the river.

Kundi My lady!

Oyebisi *turns to see that* **Kundi** *is still under* **Awosika**'s *spell. She grabs* **Awosika**'s *amulet and taps* **Kundi** *with it.* **Kundi** *crows like a cock, flapping his arms.* **Oyebisi** *drops* **Awosika**'s *amulet and uses her amulet.*

Oyebisi Is Woman not an orisa? Does water not weather the stone? Whatever spell Awosika has bound you with, release him. I, Oyebisi, I say release him!

Kundi *is released from the spell. He bends over, breathless.*

Oyebisi Be quick, ah!

Kundi *drags* **Awosika**'s *body away.* **Oyebisi** *looks around the shrine, breathless at her deeds. She composes herself and leaves the shrine. Sunlight breaks through the dark clouds.*

Oyebisi   Aderemi, the path is clear. Now let us stride together towards our destiny!

Oyebisi *exits.* **Arokin** *enters.*

Arokin   Never in living memory had a babalawo been murdered. Fingers were pointed at the fleeing Fulani soldiers. I saw Awosika's despoiled sacrifice. But I cannot record my suspicions as fact.

Iyanifa, **Awosika**'s *sister and fellow diviner, enters, mourning.*

Arokin   Iyanifa, Awosika's sister and fellow diviner, came from her sacred grove to perform a cleansing ritual. It was rumoured that before departing Oyo, she cursed . . .

Iyanifa (*tearfully*)   The child that will not let their mother sleep also will not sleep. Whoever has laid my brother to an early rest, that person will not rest. He who drinks blood shall urinate blood.

Scene Four

A week later. The Alaafin's palace. **Aderemi, Arokin, Iwalagba, Adekanbi, Opaleye, Iya Agan, Afilaka, Ashabi, Ashadele,** *courtiers, etc.* **Ayan** *drums as* **Aderemi** *prostrates before* **Iwalagba**. **Afilaka** *looks contemptuously at* **Aderemi**. **Opaleye** *holds the staff of office of* **Aare Ona Kakanfo** *for* **Iwalagba** *to hand over to* **Aderemi**.

All   Kabiyesi!

Iwalagba   Aderemi Ajanaku, son of Ajasa. Your name will live on as one who saved the empire with your courage.

All   *Ase!*

Ayan   Kabiyesi, oh!

Iwalagba To celebrate this victory that has perpetuated our glorious reign, in ten market days, we will hold the Bebe Festival.

Ayan *stops drumming. Hushed concern.*

Opaleye Kabiyesi, are you certain of this?

Iwalagba Iya Agan.

Iya Agan Kabiyesi.

Iwalagba Make sure the King's Masquerader arrives on time.

Iya Agan Eh, Kabiyesi, there is a reason Bebe is nicknamed the Festival of Death. Two of your predecessors died during the festival.

Afilaka Your father dared not hold Bebe.

Iwalagba And yet, did he not die a mere seven months into his reign?

Opaleye The portends were there.

Iwalagba Let us not fear the future because of what happened in the past.

Afilaka Kabiyesi, the past is our guide to the future.

Iwalagba Arokin, what does history tell us?

Arokin Past kings have celebrated Bebe without mishap. It is the festival appropriate for this moment, where the rich and poor are equal and where the Alaafin supplicates his predecessors to ensure a long and prosperous reign. Oluawo Awosika's advice to guarantee a successful festival is in need . . .

Opaleye (*raises his hand to cut off* **Arokin**) Arokin . . .

Arokin . . . His shrine was far from the battlefield.

Afilaka A local could not have committed such a sacrilege.

Iwalagba The festival will hold.

Opaleye   Your highness /

Adekanbi   The King has spoken.

Aderemi *is in pain.* **Ashadele** *tries to alert* **Iwalagba** *to* **Aderemi***'s discomfort.*

Opaleye   Whenever you open your mouth I long for the days when the king died, the crown prince had to die with him.

Adekanbi   Basorun, *ko ni da fun e.*[18]

Iya Agan   Adekanbi!

Opaleye   *Baba re ni ko ni da fun, iwo omo komo buruku yi!*[19]

Opaleye *remembers* **Iwalagba** *is* **Adekanbi***'s father, prostrates before* **Iwalagba**.

Opaleye   Forgive me, Kabiyesi. Your riff-raff son behaves like he does not know the meaning of your name.

Adekanbi   Your family will die!

Opaleye *and* **Adekanbi** *hurl insults and curses at each other.*

Ashadele (*points to* **Aderemi**)   Kabiyesi!

Opaleye *and* **Aderemi** *stop arguing.*

Iwalagba   Ah, Aare Aderemi, rise, please rise.

Aderemi *rises, stiff.* **Opaleye** *hands* **Iwalagba** *the staff of office who then hands it to* **Aderemi**.

Opaleye   All hail, Aderemi, Aare Ona Kakanfo!

All   Hail!

A ceremonial song and dance. **Ashadele**, *laughing, tries to cheer up* **Aderemi**. *Everyone dances off except for* **Aderemi**. *He stands, angry and humiliated as the scene changes around him.* **Oyebisi** *enters.*

---

18 Damn you.
19 Damn your father, you errant child.

Scene Five

Later that day. Night. The bedchamber of **Aderemi***'s house in Ilara, a province of Oyo.* **Oyebisi** *helps* **Aderemi** *take off his clothes and massages his shoulders.*

Aderemi I was left prostrating like a lizard on the day honour should have been accorded to me! Oh, did I wish there and then that I was Alaafin. I would have given them something to remember me by.

Oyebisi Why do you wish for a day that is coming?

Aderemi With Awosika gone, the chicken's wings have been plucked before it attempts to fly.

Oyebisi Awosika was Ifa's mouthpiece. He wielded no power himself.

Aderemi My wife, let me be satisfied with Aare . . . I know this seems small to you. I have tried to give you the life of a queen.

Oyebisi It is not the same as being queen.

Aderemi *looks deflated.* **Oyebisi** *hugs him.*

Oyebisi You have done more than a king could do for me. You have stayed with me and not taken another wife even though the world wonders why. People say I have bewitched you, that I have tied you down and who will inherit your estate.

Aderemi Are you sure you have not had Ayebami cast a spell on me?

Oyebisi My lord!

Aderemi *laughs, hugs* **Oyebisi**.

Aderemi Let us enjoy our good fortune and continue trying for a child. Awosika told me of a babalawo in Ile-Ife.

Oyebisi I am tired of drinking potions, performing rituals and sleeping in sacred groves. Am I worthless if I am without child?

Aderemi *holds her hands in his hands.*

Aderemi Not to me, my love. In your heart your desire to avenge your family remains strong. But see how the gods have compensated you with wealth and status. Yes, we would trade all of this for a child but we should not be like the tortoise and claim food that was meant for the community for only ourselves.

Oyebisi Why are you fighting your destiny when the gods show you the way?

Aderemi Speak clearly, Oyebisi.

Oyebisi The Bebe Festival.

Aderemi What of it?

Oyebisi *gives* **Aderemi** *a look like he should know what she means.*

Aderemi What if Iwalagba doesn't meet with misfortune?

Oyebisi We will see to it that he does.

Aderemi Oyebisi! Sacrilege!

Oyebisi How many Alaafins did Basorun Gaa[20] send to their deaths? And how many crown princes poisoned their fathers to ascend the throne? Is that not how Iwalagba became Alaafin?

Aderemi That is hearsay.

Oyebisi I lived in a palace. I know what games these lords play and how they pronounce the will of mute gods to justify their actions.

---

20 Powerful prime minister of the Oyo Empire from the seventeenth to the eighteenth century.

Aderemi My heart trembles at the thought of what you insinuate. The Alaafin is second only to the *orisas*.

Oyebisi You have shed the blood of warriors, nobles and commoners. Can you distinguish between them? During Bebe, are king and commoner not equal? Why then does my lord fear words? You saved Oyo yet the court despises you. It despises us. To them, you will always be nothing more than the son of a blacksmith. Oh, you think Ashadele's mirth was a gesture of brotherhood?

Aderemi The council chose me over him. Do not bring division between me and my friend.

Oyebisi You are friends in the way a rich man is a friend to a pauper. Have you ever heard a hawk call an elephant his best friend?

A **Servant** *enters, followed by* **Ashadele**.

Servant My lord, Balogun Ashadele.

Aderemi Ah, Ashadele.

Aderemi *puts on his garment.* **Oyebisi** *comes out and kneels before* **Ashadele**.

Oyebisi Welcome, Balogun.

Ashadele Oyebisi. How are you?

Oyebisi I am fine, my lord. How are the twins?

Ashadele It pains me to be away from them for too long. The gods will grant you your own bundles of joy.

Aderemi *enters from his bedchamber.*

Aderemi My friend and brother.

Ashadele Aare Ona Kakanfo. The title fits you.

Oyebisi As it should.

Aderemi My wife, please leave us.

Ashadele My lady.

Oyebisi *curtseys and leaves. She eavesdrops on their conversation.*

Ashadele You must install your replacement as soon as possible. There are several commanders of great lineage to choose from.

Aderemi Lineage does not make a warrior.

Ashadele It makes the man.

Aderemi And what does it make of me, brother?

Ashadele It makes you the Elephant.

Aderemi You have spoken well.

Ashadele You know me, my brother. I do not deal in insinuation.

Aderemi It is your honesty and straightforwardness I treasure the most.

Ashadele And I yours.

Aderemi What are your thoughts on Iwalagba holding Bebe?

Ashadele What do you mean?

Aderemi Do you not think it is reckless timing?

Ashadele That is a matter for the Oyomesi.

Aderemi It was Iwalagba's war of expansion which led to the Ekiti revolt, that left our northern borders exposed to the Fulani attack.

Ashadele It has always been the custom that the Aare pays the price for failure.

Aderemi You see our victory as failure?

Ashadele It was Ogunwolu's fate.

Aderemi Who ordained his fate? Was it Ifa or Kabiyesi?

Ashadele You have never questioned Kabiyesi before. What troubles you?

Scene Five

Aderemi You know me too well, brother . . . Awosika told me . . .

Oyebisi *barges in.*

Oyebisi Balogun Ashadele, my husband has had a long day. Call upon him tomorrow when he is rested.

Ashadele I cannot argue with the lady of the house. Aare, I take my leave.

Aderemi Tomorrow, Ashadele.

Ashadele *exits.*

Oyebisi Aderemi, are Ifa's words not enough for you? Is my advice not enough?

Aderemi I needed a man's advice.

Oyebisi I am worth ten men.

Aderemi I do not doubt that.

Oyebisi And of all the men, it is Ashadele who I warned you of that you turn to.

Aderemi Forgive me.

Oyebisi For our safety, no one outside this room is your friend until our mission succeeds.

Aderemi To become Alaafin requires the trust of people.

Oyebisi Which person dare oppose that which is ordained by the gods?

Adebisi Without man there can be no gods. Is this not what you always tell me?

Oyebisi You have faced death a thousand times. Your sword is stronger than anything those bigots in court wield and yet all I hear from you is fear and doubt! What is it you really fear, Aderemi? Show me and I will confront it!

Aderemi You are right! Ifa says it is my destiny. If it is king I will be, then king I must be. I will be king with you as my queen.

Oyebisi Now you speak like the man I married!

Aderemi Iwalagba will not be alone. I must find the right time to strike.

Oyebisi You intend to use your sword?

Aderemi I am a soldier. I must look my adversary in the eye when I strike him dead.

Oyebisi You do not mean to strike him in public.

Aderemi Is it not ordained that I shall be Alaafin?

Oyebisi There is a reason why the tortoise outlives the fowl.

Aderemi Ehn?

Oyebisi I have a more discreet plan. First, we must prepare. Ayebami!

Ayebami *enters.*

Oyebisi Fortify my husband.

Aderemi I do not need fortification from your wizard. Awosika shored me with power that will make Ogun himself hesitate to challenge me to combat.

Oyebisi Awosika is gone.

Aderemi *hesitates.*

Oyebisi (*reassuring*) Ayebami will supplement Awosika's spells. *Oya*,[21] Ayebami.

Ayebami *performs a ritual on* **Aderemi**. **Aderemi** *responds through movement as the power courses through his body. As the ritual progresses, he gets stronger.*

---

21 Get going.

Oyebisi From this moment onwards, no man shall be superior to you.

Aderemi No man . . .

Oyebisi You will bow to no man.

Aderemi No man . . .

Oyebisi Aderemi, who are you?

Aderemi I am Kabiyesi.

Oyebisi Aderemi Ajanaku, I cannot hear you!

Aderemi I am Kabiyesi!

Oyebisi Louder!

Aderemi I am Kabiyesi.

Oyebisi *kneels,* **Ayebami** *prostrates.*

Oyebisi/Ayebami *Iku Baba Yeye!*

Scene Six

A few weeks later. The Bebe Festival. **Iya Ayan** *leads* **Iwalagba***'s procession.* **Iya Agan** *directs the* **Masquerades** *as she anxiously looks out for someone. At an opportune moment* **Aderemi** *makes to unsheathe his sword but* **Oyebisi** *stops him. The procession exits except for* **Iya Agan**. **Arokin** *enters, panting.*

Arokin I searched everywhere. I met Adekanbi cavorting with a woman.

Iya Agan We cannot proceed to the *Bara*[22] without the King's Masquerade. Iwalagba cannot beat the Bebe drum to begin the festival.

Oyebisi *enters.*

Oyebisi Iya Agan, we are waiting for you.

---

22 The burial place of kings, where the previous kings are buried.

Iya Agan Arokin, wait here in case he turns up.

Arokin I am missing the proceedings. Do you know how hard it is to construct a truthful account from second-hand sources?

Arokin *starts walking away.*

Iya Agan Just a little more time, Arokin. He will soon be here.

Arokin He is your responsibility.

Voice (*off; angrily*) Iya Agan!

Oyebisi I will wait for him.

Arokin *Yi o da fun yin.*[23]

Arokin *exits after the procession.*

Iya Agan Thank you, my daughter. When he arrives, get him prepared and bring him to the *Bara*.

Iya Agan *exits.* **Aderemi** *enters.*

Aderemi You place food before a hungry man but you say he must not consume it.

Oyebisi The King's Masquerader is late. Iya Agan has asked me to take him to the *Bara*. When he arrives, I will give him a sleeping potion before I take him there. You will steal away from the procession to the *Bara* and kill Iwalagba where his predecessors sleep, then you will place the knife in the Masquerader's hand.

Aderemi To kill Iwalagba in the *Bara*? Is this transgression not too much for any man?

Oyebisi Ayebami has fortified you against any repercussion.

---

23 A blessing.

Aderemi The masquerades are manifestations of our ancestors. What if no one believes he did it?

Oyebisi While he gets ready, I will plant evidence in the masquerades' compound. This is our turn, my husband. Think only of what comes after the deed is done.

The **King's Masquerader** *dashes in.*

King's Masquerader I am late!

Oyebisi Have a drink to calm your nerves.

Oyebisi *gives him the potion. He downs it.*

Oyebisi Let's get you prepared. Your king awaits you.

The **King's Masquerader** *exits hastily.*

Oyebisi (*to* **Aderemi**) Play your part, my lord, and you will hunger no more.

Scene Seven

The King's Bara. A solemn drumbeat accompanies the eerie moaning of the **Late Kings** *buried there. The* gbedu[24] *is to one side. Entranced,* **Iwalagba** *ceremonially washes his hair while the* **King's Masquerade***, combatting the effects of the potion, struggles to stay awake. The sky darkens as* **Aderemi** *and* **Oyebisi** *enter.* **Oyebisi** *has her dagger in her hand.*

Oyebisi How I wish I could drive the dagger into his stomach.

Aderemi It is enough that your weapon shall do the killing. (*Looks up at the sky.*) Is it my eyes or is the sky darkening?

The moans of the **Late Kings***. Only* **Aderemi** *can hear it.*

Aderemi And that sound.

Oyebisi What sound, my lord?

---

24 The Big Drum, used for state occasions.

Aderemi Can you not hear it? It chills my spirit.

Oyebisi Do not let fear rob you of your momentum. Ifa has ordained it. Your amulets will grant you passage over the threshold of the *Bara*.

Oyebisi *hovers her amulet over her dagger and whispers an incantation. As she hands* **Aderemi** *the dagger, she clasps his hands in hers.*

Oyebisi I am with you, my husband.

They press their foreheads together. **Aderemi** *goes to the threshold of the* Bara. *He kisses his amulet and steps forward. Drumbeat as* **Aderemi** *battles the elemental forces threatening to tear him to shreds. The moaning of the* **Late Kings** *gets louder with each step he takes.* **Iwalagba** *falls into a trance. The* **King's Masquerade** *totters from the effects of the potion.*

Aderemi This noise is deafening!

Oyebisi Go forth, Aderemi!

Aderemi I cannot hear you, Oyebisi!

Oyebisi Who can withstand the Elephant's stampede? Aderemi Ajanaku, go forth, I say!

With a monumental effort of will, **Aderemi** *crosses the threshold just as the* **King's Masquerade** *falls to the ground asleep.* **Iwalagba** *is oblivious of what is going on. He picks up the drumsticks. As he is about to beat the* gbedu, *to his surprise he sees* **Aderemi**. **Iwalagba** *and the* **Late Kings** *cry out simultaneously as* **Aderemi** *stabs him – it is as if he is stabbing the generations of kings buried there. Sango's thunderbolt tears a hole in the sky.*

Iwalagba *grabs at* **Aderemi**, *tearing off his necklace before dying.* **Aderemi** *retrieves the necklace but one of the amulets is in* **Iwalagba**'s *hand.* **Aderemi** *places the dagger in the hand of the* **King's Masquerade** *and comes out of the* Bara, *breathless, his hands trembling.*

Aderemi It is done.

Oyebisi My ancestors, you are avenged.

Aderemi See how my hands tremble.

Oyebisi *presses his hands with her hands.*

Oyebisi The gods are on our side. We must rejoin the procession before suspicion is attached to our disappearance.

Oyebisi *leads* **Aderemi** *offstage.*

Lightning. A dirge.

Moments later. **Arokin**, **Opaleye**, **Ashadele** *and* **Iya Agan** *enter, followed by* **Aderemi** *and* **Oyebisi**.

Opaleye The last time I saw a thunderbolt was when Iwalagba's father died.

Ashadele Let us not imprint on the future the tragedy of the past.

Opaleye (*calls*) Kabiyesi! We have not heard the drum . . .

Silence.

Iya Agan Kabiyesi, oh!

Adekanbi *enters, laughing with a* **Woman**.

Opaleye Where have you been?

Ashadele (*to the* **Woman**) Begone!

The **Woman** *makes to leave.* **Adekanbi** *holds her defiantly.*

Adekanbi (*to the* **Woman**) Stay!

Iya Agan Your father is still in the *Bara*.

Adekanbi What is he still doing in there?

Opaleye *claps his hands in disgust as* **Adekanbi** *enters the* Bara.

Adekanbi Father? Father . . . Father!

Aderemi *dashes in, followed by the others.*

Adekanbi They have killed my father!

*The **Woman** takes to her heels. **Aderemi** draws his sword.*

Aderemi   Let no one enter the *Bara*!

Ashadele   Who would dare commit such a taboo?

Ashadele *prises* **Aderemi***'s amulet from* **Iwalagba***'s hand. Recognising it, he makes to show* **Aderemi** *when the* **King's Masquerade** *stirs.*

Aderemi   Look here! The murderer!

Iya Agan   Aare, wait . . . Wait!

Aderemi *kills the* **King's Masquerade**.

Iya Agan   Aderemi!

Iya Agan *rushes to the* **King's Masquerade**. **Ashadele** *pockets the amulet.*

Iya Agan   Why did you do that!

Oyebisi *and* **Kundi** *enter.*

Oyebisi   I heard screaming.

Arokin   Kabiyesi is slain.

Iya Agan   He killed the King's Masquerade!

Aderemi   He killed Kabiyesi!

Opaleye   We cannot say for certain.

Aderemi   The knife was in his hand! What other proof do we need?

Ashadele   Oyebisi, you escorted the King's Masquerade to the *Bara*. Did you see anything untoward?

Oyebisi   I /

Aderemi   She saw nothing.

Ashadele (*to* **Oyebisi**)   Are you sure/

Oyebisi (*pretends to faint*)   The Bebe curse!

Arokin *runs to aid* **Oyebisi**.

Aderemi He could not have done it alone. He must have had help from the other masqueraders.

Iya Agan That is nonsense! They have been at their posts.

Aderemi Kundi!

Kundi (*off*) My lord!

Aderemi Round up the masqueraders!

Kundi Yes, my lord!

Iya Agan They are my responsibility!

Iya Agan *makes to go after* **Kundi**. **Ashadele** *stops her and runs after* **Kundi**.

Aderemi Aremo Adekanbi, where were you?

Adekanbi *is petrified*.

Opaleye As prime minister, I shall conduct the investigation.

Aderemi Your laxness caused Iwalagba to stray from our customs.

Opaleye I have been prime minister to four kings.

Aderemi Two of whom died prematurely.

Offstage the **Masqueraders** *plead their innocence*. **Ashadele** *enters, with a bloodied piece of masquerade material. He gives it to* **Iya Agan**.

Ashadele Kundi says he found this bloody cloth on them. They swear they have never seen it.

Iya Agan There must be another reason . . .

Opaleye I will question them . . .

Aderemi *storms towards the* **Masqueraders**. **Ashadele** *blocks his path*.

Ashadele Aderemi.

Aderemi Step aside.

Ashadele Let Basorun administer the law. This is not justice.

Iya Agan Wait . . .

Aderemi Your Aare commands you to step aside!

Ashadele *moves out of* **Aderemi**'s *way.*

Iya Agan Aare, wait!

Iya Agan *hurries after him.* **Aderemi** *exits. Screams. Those onstage recoil as* **Aderemi** *kills the* **Masqueraders**. **Adekanbi** *makes to flee.*

Adekanbi I am not waiting for him to kill me.

Arokin Who will bury your father?

Adekanbi Have you seen a dead son bury his father?

Opaleye Run to Ile-Ife. Seek refuge with Our Mother Moremi. Hurry!

Adekanbi *flees. The final scream, of a boy, is heard.* **Aderemi** *enters, his sword and arms bloodied.*

Aderemi Justice is served. My king is avenged.

Oyebisi *goes to* **Aderemi** *and puts her arms around him.* **Iya Agan** *enters singing a dirge. The drumbeat gets louder as everyone around freezes in horror and fear at the bloody sight of* **Aderemi** *and* **Oyebisi**. *The chilling sound of a dog weeping.*

Darkness. **Aderemi** *and* **Oyebisi**, *alone onstage. She wipes the blood off* **Aderemi** *with her hands – they are both now covered in blood.* **Ayebami** *emerges from the darkness and cleans their hands with a cloth, mouthing incantations as he guides them offstage.*

Arokin *enters.*

Arokin Strange sightings are reported since Iwalagba's murder. Tutuola, the palm-wine tapper, swore he saw a gorilla with a tortoise shell. Oyeyemi the weaver saw a woman with elephant tusks and vipers for hair cradling an antelope as if it were her child. Fagunwa the hunter claimed spirits have used magic to dry up the forests. The Oyomesi have sent Gboun-Gboun to Ile-Ife to consult the oracle. In the meantime, they have requested that the seven royal houses from whom kings are chosen to meet with them to decide what step to take /

A **Soldier** *enters.*

Soldier You are breaking the curfew!

Arokin I'm on my way home, sir.

Soldier Move!

Cowering, **Arokin** *exits.*

Scene Eight

A few days later. The palace throne room. **Opaleye**, **Iya Agan**, **Ashabi** *and* **Afilaka**.

Ashabi An Alaafin murdered in the *Bara. Enu ko gbodo so.*[25] What will unborn generations think of us?

Opaleye If word of this abomination spreads the empire will unravel.

Iya Agan The ancestral masquerades slain like chickens. Who will escort Iwalagba to the other side?

Afilaka It is our fault for promoting a man of common stock.

Iya Agan My family is of 'common stock'. Do you see me acting in such a manner?

---

25 Unspeakable.

*A **Servant** enters. He shakes his head and exits.*

Opaleye We have given the royal houses enough time to meet with us.

Ashabi The four houses that demand Aderemi stand trial will come. Give them more time.

Iya Agan Four out of seven houses? No. We need all of them to act as one.

Opaleye We must decide what to do about Aderemi without them.

Ashabi I support the four houses. Aderemi must stand trial.

Afilaka Of course you support them. They promised you they would end the custom that requires you to die with Kabiyesi.

Ashabi I knew it! You want me to die.

Afilaka I have no ill will towards you. Tradition demands it.

Iya Agan Have we not had enough killing?

Afilaka These strange sightings are because Samu Ashabi has not performed his duty. They are a warning of worse to come for Oyo if he does not go to serve Iwalagba. As far as I am concerned, Ashabi, you are a corpse.

Ashabi Me, a corpse! What of Aderemi who is responsible for all this?

Opaleye Given the events of these past few days, we need calm heads.

Iya Agan Did Aderemi show a calm head when he murdered the embodiments of our ancestors? The wailing of their families haunts me night and day.

Ashabi I say we arrest him now!

Afilaka Eh, go and arrest him.

Ashabi Oh, you think I can't?

Iya Agan The King's Masquerader had only just taken a new wife. How do I face his widow?

Opaleye We have more pressing matters to worry about than avenge the death of a newlywed who turned up late to an important ceremony.

Iya Agan Basorun!

Opaleye I do not mean to be harsh, Iya Agan, but it is a matter of priorities. Adekanbi's fleeing has complicated matters. If one of the royal houses came forward, we could appoint their prince as Alaafin and pass over Adekanbi.

Afilaka Which one of them would want to reign with Aderemi as their Aare? They will be as powerless as the Alaafins under Basorun Gaa.

Opaleye The empire cannot be without a head for too long.

Afilaka (*to* **Opaleye**) We would not be in this state if you hadn't ceded to Iwalagba appointing Aderemi just like you have done on every other matter.

Opaleye Upon reflection I should have been firmer with Iwalagba. He was like a son to me.

Afilaka The only way to calm our people is to be firm in following our customs.

Opaleye Firm but not inflexible.

Afilaka Why do you deem standing by our customs inflexible? Would you have me try to get out of performing my duty like this coward Ashabi?

Ashabi Afilaka, I'm warning you!

Opaleye My lords . . .

The **Servant** *enters.*

Servant Basorun, Aare Aderemi seeks your audience.

Ashabi (*scared*) He is here? What does he want?

Afilaka Send him away. He is not a member of the Oyomesi.

Opaleye He is head of our armed forces who ordered a curfew without seeking our permission.

Afilaka (*to the* **Servant**) Tell him no.

Opaleye (*to the* **Servant**) Let him in.

Afilaka Basorun!

Iya Agan He has no business here . . .

Aderemi *enters in full combat attire.*

Aderemi My lords and lady, I greet you.

Ashabi Ah, Aare Aderemi. Welcome.

Ashabi *prostrates and fetches a stool for* **Aderemi**, *shooing away the* **Servant**. *The* **Servant** *exits.* **Aderemi** *stays standing.*

Aderemi Forgive me for imposing the curfew without consulting you. I had to maintain order. I am pleased it has not impeded you from carrying out your duties.

Opaleye We must continue to administer the empire.

Aderemi I understand that Gboun-Gboun has not yet returned from Ile-Ife.

Ashabi We still wait his arrival.

Iya Agan Is that what brings you here uninvited? You could have sent a servant.

Aderemi I am aware that my presence is not in keeping with the separation of powers as our customs mandate.

Afilaka And yet here you are, in full military attire.

Aderemi We are in unusual times. The situation demands that I dress the part.

Iya Agan You executed my wards without evidence.

Aderemi Would you have them alive to put the suspicion on you? Or did you not see how all eyes fell on Adekanbi when there was less evidence of his involvement in his father's death?

Iya Agan What are you accusing me of?

Aderemi I accuse you of nothing. I merely state the obvious which you with your advanced years seem ignorant of.

Iya Agan Oh, I should thank you for making children fatherless and women widows? These people were under my patronage! They were citizens of Oyo.

Aderemi I did what any soldier loyal to his king would have done.

Afilaka I said it that Ashadele should succeed Ogunwolu!

Ashabi Not me, oh!

Afilaka Ashadele himself said he did not have the sophistication to be Aare.

Iya Agan (*aghast at* **Afilaka**'s *indiscretion*) Ah!

Opaleye Agbaakin Afilaka . . .

Afilaka I vote to remove Aderemi as Aare and replace him with Ashadele.

Opaleye Agbaakin Afilaka. Need I remind you, who stands on custom and tradition, that our deliberations are meant to be kept secret?

Afilaka And what custom and tradition are you standing on that you granted him audience with us?

Opaleye Afilaka!

Afilaka *seethes but holds his tongue.*

Opaleye (*to* **Aderemi**)   Aare, what is on your mind?

Aderemi   Thank you, Basorun. Given how Iwalagba died, to take this long to appoint a successor is a dereliction of duty, especially when the gods have spoken.

Opaleye   Spoken to whom?

Aderemi   You are consulting with the royal houses.

Ashabi   No, oh . . .

Afilaka   We are doing what tradition demands.

Aderemi   Tradition will not defend us from our enemies once they discover we are a body without a head.

Opaleye   What does the Aare propose?

Aderemi   There are reports of daily attacks by the Fulani on our northern borders. The Ekiti will soon announce their secession /

Basorun   What do you propose?

Aderemi   Make me Alaafin.

The **Oyomesi** *react with amazement.* **Afilaka** *claps his hands in disgust.*

Afilaka (*mocking laughter*)   Hey! I have seen something today! You, Aderemi, you want to stain the throne with your sooty blacksmith's bottom?

Basorun   Agbaakin . . .

Afilaka   You really believe that you and Oyebisi, a former slave, will rule over us?

Ashabi   Let us reason /

Afilaka   Tell us. How would Ifa sanction you, a murderer, as our Alaafin?

Aderemi Oh, but if the wastrel and philanderer Adekanbi had not fled, you would have placed the crown on his head. Or did Ifa sanction it before Iwalagba decreed his son should succeed him?

Afilaka Better him than you. You will disgrace Oyo over my dead body!

Afilaka *storms out.*

Iya Agan Agbaakin Afilaka!

Aderemi I leave you to deliberate on my proposal. Don't leave it too long. It does not bode well to disobey the gods.

Ashabi Kabiyesi, oh!

Ashabi *prostrates and follows* **Aderemi**. *They exit.*

Iya Agan What does he mean by this?

Opaleye We must tread carefully. But even an elephant can fall into the hunter's trap.

A crossroads near Oyo. **Kundi** *lies in wait.* **Gboun-Gboun** *enters walking back from Ile-Ife.* **Kundi** *hails* **Gboun-Gboun** *and offers him a gourd of water which* **Gboun-Gboun** *gratefully accepts. As he hands back the gourd,* **Kundi** *grabs him and drags him offstage.*

Scene Nine

That same day. **Ashadele**'s *farm.* **Ashadele** *uproots a dried-up yam.* **Arokin** *drinks from a calabash of palm wine. A* **Spy** *watches them from a distance. They act casually.*

Arokin A witness claims he saw an elephant with the wings of a hawk flying towards the sun. The wings caught fire causing it to plunge into River Osun.

Ashadele Do you have new evidence?

Arokin Oyebisi summoned Ayan and me to 'revise' their history. I said I record the truth. She dismissed me but asked Ayan to stay. As I left, Ayebami walked in.

Ashadele Awosika banished him and forbade him from calling himself babalawo.

Arokin Yes, yes, but hear this. They spoke of a missing amulet.

Turning his back to the **Spy**, **Ashadele** *brings out* **Aderemi**'s *amulet from his pouch and shows it to* **Arokin**.

Ashadele I found this on Iwalagba. It belongs to Aderemi.

Arokin This must be it! You must inform the Oyomesi!

Ashadele (*glances at the* **Spy**) Arokin . . .

Arokin *gestures an apology for raising his voice. They draw closer to each other.*

Ashadele I will tell Opaleye.

Arokin What do you want me to do?

Ashadele You are the court historian. Keep recording the truth.

Scene Ten

That same day, night. **Aderemi**'s *house.* **Oyebisi** *watches* **Aderemi** *pace around furiously.*

Aderemi Gboun-Gboun should have arrived with a message from the oracle since yesterday. They are hiding him to prevent me from becoming Alaafin.

Oyebisi They fear you too much to play such a dangerous game.

Aderemi Should a king's head be naked when Ifa has promised him the crown?

Oyebisi Patience, my lord.

Aderemi This journey began with your dream, yet I am plagued with nightmares of silence. I am doing the bidding of the gods. Why then do my ancestors not speak to me when I seek answers in this matter? Are they angry that I want to rewrite my history? None of them has reached the heights that I have reached.

Oyebisi If you consult Ayebami /

Aderemi He is not a babalawo!

Oyebisi Awosika who banned him is no more. If you do not believe in Ayebami, believe in the gods. The crown is not a bone that is thrown to a dog.

Arokin *enters.*

Oyebisi Arokin. Have you changed your mind?

Arokin I have a message for Aare Aderemi.

Aderemi Gboun-Gboun has returned!

Arokin No, Aare. The message is from the Oyomesi.

Oyebisi You see, my lord? They have come to their senses.

Aderemi Speak.

Arokin The Oyomesi confirms you as Regent until a new Alaafin is appointed /

Aderemi Ehn? Did you say Regent?

Arokin Yes, my lord.

Aderemi (*to* **Oyebisi**) You said they are not playing games with me! (*To* **Arokin**.) Tell Basorun Opaleye, Aderemi will not be a caretaker /

Oyebisi Tell him that Aare Aderemi accepts the role.

Aderemi What?

Oyebisi You may leave us.

Arokin *exits.*

Aderemi Why!

Oyebisi My lord, you will have administrative authority. Combined with your military power, you are Alaafin in all but name.

Aderemi This is not what the prophecy promised me!

Oyebisi Awosika said the path is a crossroad. Patience, my lord.

Aderemi 'Patience', she says! 'Patience, patience, patience'! Is it because you have got your revenge that your favourite word is now 'patience'?

Oyebisi No, my lord.

Aderemi Then tell me, why is Oyo without a king yet no crown adorns my head? (*Remembers.*) Ah! Awosika told me to sacrifice to Esu! How have I forgotten? Ayebami!

Aderemi *exits.* **Ayebami** *enters.* **Esu** *appears.*

Ayebami My lord called.

Oyebisi He wants to sacrifice to Esu.

Esu *laughs.* **Kundi** *enters.*

Kundi It is done, my lady. Gboun-Gboun is dead.

Oyebisi Did you extract the oracle's message from him?

Kundi He put up a struggle . . .

Ayebami The Oyomesi will send another messenger to Ile-Ife.

Kundi He will meet the same fate as Gboun-Gboun.

Aderemi (*off*) Ayebami!

Ayebami What should I say to my lord?

Oyebisi Tell him Esu says patience is the king of virtues. Convince him that the gods speak through you, and I will return to you what Awosika took from you and more.

Ayebami *exits.* **Oyebisi** *looks worried.* **Esu** *looks bemused at* **Oyebisi** *and exits.*

Ayan *enters drumming into Scene Eleven.*

Scene Eleven

The next day. The Alaafin's palace. The investiture of **Aderemi** *as Adele.*[26] *The court includes* **Iya Agan** *who keeps watch over a glowering* **Afilaka, Ashabi, Ashadele, Arokin** *and* **Citizens** *of Oyo. To everyone's surprise* **Ayebami** *enters wearing* **Awosika's** *uniform of Chief of Oyo Diviners, daring anyone to oppose him.* **Oyebisi** *stands beside* **Aderemi** *as* **Opaleye***, holding the regent's staff of office, presides over the ceremony.* **Aderemi** *eyes the throne, his desire clear to see.*

Iwalagba's Ghost *enters wearing a blood red crown.* **Ayebami** *performs a ritual then hands the proceedings back to* **Opaleye***.*

Opaleye Thank you, Ayebami.

Ayebami *Oluawo* Ayebami, my lord /

Opaleye Aare Aderemi, I hand to you the staff of office of Regent until the Oyomesi selects a new Alaafin in accordance with our customs. Henceforth you will go by the title of Adele Aderemi and be known by all throughout the empire as such . . .

Aderemi *is about to take the staff when he sees* **Iwalagba's Ghost***.*

Opaleye Aare, the staff . . .

Aderemi Are you not dead?

Everyone reacts with confusion.

---

26 Regent.

Opaleye Er, I am very much alive?

Aderemi Are you deaf and dumb? I said are you not dead?

Opaleye Aare /

Oyebisi He was not talking to you, Basorun. Excuse us.

Kundi Make way!

Oyebisi *draws* **Aderemi** *aside.*

Oyebisi My husband, what is it?

Aderemi Can you not see him?

Oyebisi See who?

Aderemi There!

Oyebisi (*looks in the direction of* **Iwalagba's Ghost**) My husband /

Aderemi LOOK!

Oyebisi Look at who?

Aderemi (*to* **Ayebami**) I reward you with Awosika's position, and you perform your wizardry on me!

Ayebami I have done no such thing, my lord.

Aderemi (*to* **Iwalagba's Ghost**) What blood still flows from your wounds? Away from me!

Oyebisi There is nobody there! Compose yourself. People are watching.

Oyebisi *leads* **Aderemi** *back to the ceremony. The* **Courtiers** *and* **Citizens** *quieten.* **Iwalagba's Ghost** *fades into the background.*

Oyebisi Apologies, lords and ladies.

Oyebisi *shoves* **Aderemi** *back into position.*

Opaleye Aare, is everything all right?

Oyebisi *Adele* Aderemi is fine.

Aderemi The staff.

Opaleye *hands* **Aderemi** *the staff of office.* **Iwalagba's Ghost** *reappears and sits on the throne.*

Opaleye Now for the /

Aderemi Are you mocking me?

Opaleye Did I say something to offend you?

Aderemi Your carcass is only keeping that seat warm. I fear no man living or dead!

Iya Agan Aare Aderemi!

Iwalagba's Ghost *offers* **Aderemi** *the crown.*

Aderemi How dare you offer me a crown of blood? Who are you to obstruct the will of the gods?

Opaleye Aare Aderemi!

Oyebisi The Adele is battling a fever. He hid it to play his part in restoring order to Oyo.

Ayebami I will treat him after the ceremony.

Oyebisi Please, continue.

Opaleye Swear on the staff.

Aderemi *(composes himself)* . . . I swear by the gods to uphold the laws of the land and protect the empire from enemies at home and abroad.

All *Ase*!

Opaleye The Oyomesi has agreed that as the next in rank, Ashadele shall assume the role of Aare Ona Kakanfo.

Afilaka *grins.* **Aderemi** *laughs cynically.*

Opaleye Did I say something funny, Adele?

Aderemi I see what you are doing.

Iya Agan Adele Aderemi, you are forbidden from entering the battlefield.

Oyebisi The Alaafin is forbidden. Aderemi is regent.

Afilaka The separation of powers must still be upheld.

Aderemi What happens after you select an Alaafin? You will have two field marshals. To whom will you send the empty calabash as tradition demands?

Opaleye We will consult Ifa.

Oyebisi While Oyo is in a precarious state, we cannot afford to waste time talking endlessly like old men.

Aderemi I have spoken.

Murmurs of disapproval from the **Courtiers** *and* **Citizens**.

Afilaka No! We put an end to this madness now! Citizens of Oyo . . .!

Oyebisi *nudges* **Ayebami**.

Ayebami Citizens of Oyo! Ifa says Oyo's enemies have gotten wind of our disarray and are marching towards us.

Fear and concern run through the **Citizens**.

Citizens Another attack?

Fulani or Ekiti?

They have joined forces!

Aderemi saved us before.

Let him remain as field marshal.

Ayebami Ifa says that only Aderemi can crush our enemies.

Ashabi Who are we to oppose the oracle?

Afilaka What oracle? This charlatan is Oyebisi's stooge.

Aderemi Enough of your rudeness!

Citizens Aderemi is our hero!

Stop wasting time!

Give him what he wants!

Protect us from our enemies!

Aderemi The people have spoken. I your regent have heard you. I will protect you. The spiritual affliction must also be cured. Oluawo Ayebami consulted the oracle. Iwalagba cannot rest because we have not observed his funeral rites. It is customary for the holder of the Samu title to escort our father to the land of our ancestors. But Ifa said that from today, the Agbaakin must play that vital role.

Afilaka Ehn?

Aderemi Agbaakin Afilaka, Oyo thanks you for your service.

Ayebami Prepare him for his journey.

Afilaka No! No!

Oyebisi *smiles,* **Ashabi** *sighs with relief as* **Kundi** *and the* **Soldiers** *drag* **Afilaka** *away.* **Opaleye** *and* **Iya Agan** *look to each other, aghast.*

Aderemi (*to* **Opaleye**) Which trap is so big that it can snare the Elephant? (*To* **Iwalagba's Ghost**.) Now sleep with your ancestors and haunt me no more!

Ayan *beats his drum as* **Ayebami** *gives* **Aderemi** *a potion to drink from a gourd. All the while* **Aderemi** *cannot keep his eyes off* **Iwalagba's Ghost**. *The ritual over, dancing and singing in honour of* **Aderemi**. **Ashabi** *sings the loudest.* **Aderemi** *dances with* **Oyebisi**. **Iwalagba's Ghost** *watches their every step. The sound of a dog weeping.*

Scene Twelve

The next day. Night. A clearing inside a forest. **Opaleye** *waits. From offstage someone whistles.* **Opaleye** *whistles in response.* **Ashadele** *enters with a bundle.*

Opaleye (*sees the bundle*)   What is that?

Ashadele   I was not invited to the generals' meeting. My spy told me Aderemi intends to raise the curfew to a state of emergency and has marked the princes of the ruling houses for execution so that none can oppose his claim to the throne. If we don't leave now, we will be next.

Opaleye   Did he mention my name?

Ashadele   Basorun, why are you talking like this? I have sent word to Iya Agan. I will join Adekanbi in Ile-Ife and raise an army to thwart my old friend's ambition.

Opaleye   My wives and children.

Ashadele   If you all try to leave, you might as well sign your death warrant.

Opaleye   But to leave them behind?

Ashadele   He is not that far gone that he will harm our families. You should see him with my twins.

Opaleye   You still harbour feelings for your friend.

Ashadele   At his best he is as honourable as any nobleman. To be on opposite sides feels unnatural.

Opaleye   The Hawk and the Elephant make for an unnatural pairing.

A rustling sound.

Ashadele   Sh!

The wind shakes the tree branches.

If you are coming, we must leave now. Send word to your family to join you discreetly.

Opaleye *hesitates.*

Ashadele Basorun . . .

Opaleye . . . Lead the way.

Ashadele *exits.* **Opaleye** *look back towards Oyo.*

Ashadele (*off*) Basorun!

Opaleye (*sighs*) It is well.

Opaleye *exits after* **Ashadele**.

Scene Thirteen

The next day. Noon. The city square. The harmattan winds cover the land in a dusty haze. **Citizens of Oyo** *huddle around* **Arokin**.

Arokin (*whispers*) Citizens of Oyo, this may be the last time you hear the truth from my lips. The state of emergency has us talking in whispers . . .

Ayan *enters. The* **Citizens of Oyo** *disperse in fear.* **Arokin** *sees* **Ayan**. *As he talks,* **Ayan** *gestures to* **Arokin** *to take off his robes. They exchange clothes.*

Arokin (*loudly*) Not from fear. Everyone loves Aderemi and his sweet wife Oyebisi. We are too loud. Aderemi has found a remedy for this character fault. As a result, Oyo is prospering. The harvest is the most bounteous in recorded history. Fish fly out of the river into fishermen's nets. The sun shines night and day and it rains during harmattan. Despite the increased taxation and the daily execution of traitors, the people are so wealthy they wear clothes made of *aso oke*[27] daily to attend the funerals that are now a feature of the social calendar.

---

27 Expensive handwoven cloth.

Ayan *is now dressed as* **Arokin** *and vice versa.* **Ayan** *gives* **Arokin** *his drum and drumstick and jams his cap over* **Arokin**'s *head.*

Ayan It has been discovered by real historians like me that Aderemi is of royal blood. This means he can ascend the throne! This is a joyful day for the empire. (*To* **Arokin**.) Now beat the drum like a beggar no one will remember when you die.

Arokin *drums after* **Ayan**.

Scene Fourteen

The same day. Night. **Aderemi**'s *house in Ilara.* **Aderemi**, **Oyebisi** *with* **Kundi**.

Aderemi And Iya Agan?

Kundi She also has fled.

Aderemi Send another messenger to Ile-Ife.

Kundi (*shares a look with* **Oyebisi**) Yes, my lord.

Aderemi Tell the army to prepare.

Kundi My lord. My lady.

Kundi *exits.*

Oyebisi It is unwise to send yet another messenger to Ile-Ife now it is home to our enemies.

Aderemi Ibadan and Ijaye are sending soldiers to Opaleye! What am I supposed to do?

Oyebisi Send emissaries to the remaining kingdoms.

Aderemi Do you think I have not done so? They have heard that Ibadan and Ijaye have united against me. They say, 'We will not fight for an unlawful ruler against the two most powerful armies in the empire.' Esu showed the path to take. Why again this obstruction?

Oyebisi That is Esu's way.

Aderemi It would help if I knew what all this effort is for.

Oyebisi It is for us, my husband.

Aderemi And who reigns after me?

Oyebisi Adekanbi will never ascend the throne.

Aderemi Did I mention Adekanbi?

Oyebisi My lord /

Aderemi I have rewritten my history but what about my future?

Oyebisi Have no doubt the crown is yours . . .

Aderemi Ayan! Ayan, oh!

Ayan (*off*) My lord!

Ayan *enters.*

Aderemi What do the people say about me?

Ayan They say that you are the greatest leader /

Aderemi What do they really say? I want my wife to hear it.

Ayan (*hesitates, fearful*) Eh . . .

Aderemi The truth!

Ayan They say, and please, it is them, not me saying it!

Aderemi *approaches* **Ayan** *menacingly.*

Ayan They say, (*mimics* **Arokin**'s *voice*) 'Aderemi wants to keep the throne warm for another's dynasty. Let it not be my destiny.'

Aderemi What else do they say?

Oyebisi No need /

Aderemi (*roars*) What else?

Ayan They say, 'The blacksmith's son rewrites his history as the father of the empire but he is not even a father in his own house.'

Aderemi Thank you. Leave us.

Ayan *scurries away.*

Aderemi Do you hear that, my wife?

Oyebisi Do you think it does not eat at my heart?

Aderemi Before all this started, I asked you to go to Ile-Ife /

Oyebisi Would you like me to go there now so that our enemies can slaughter me? You do not need me to die to take another wife.

Awosika's Ghost *appears. It watches them.*

Aderemi How dare you? I've stood by you, a tree without seeds.

Kundi *enters.*

Oyebisi (*stung*) Maybe it is your seed that is rotten.

Aderemi *grabs her by the throat. She grabs his throat.*

Aderemi I will kill you!

Kundi *draws his knife.* **Oyebisi** *gestures to* **Kundi** *to stay away. He obeys reluctantly but alert to aid his mistress.*

Oyebisi Go ahead, do our enemies' work. Nothing would make them happier than to hear that you have killed me, your *orisa*. I raised you to meet your destiny! Kill me! But know that I will haunt you every night in your sleep for your weakness at letting them come between us!

Aderemi *struggles to take his hands off* **Oyebisi**'s *throat.*

Oyebisi I knew it! Our enemies are using dark forces to come between us when our victory is so close! Fight it, my lord! Fight it!

Aderemi *takes his hands off* **Oyebisi***'s throat and falls to the ground in front of her. She cradles him in her arms.* **Kundi** *sheathes his knife.* **Awosika's Ghost** *watches on.*

Oyebisi (*to* **Kundi**)   Call Ayebami.

Kundi *reluctantly exits, his eyes on* **Aderemi**.

Oyebisi   Take a wife. Take wives, so long as I am queen. Now summon that courage that made me love you. Never again show this kind of weakness.

Aderemi   I swear by all the gods, nothing shall come between us again.

Oyebisi   After all this is ended, and we are victorious, I will go to Ile-Ife.

Aderemi *stands up.* **Ayebami** *enters.* **Oyebisi** *guides* **Aderemi** *to sit on a stool.*

Ayebami   My lady. You sent for me.

Oyebisi *makes* **Aderemi** *sit upright.*

Oyebisi   Ask Ifa how the coming battle will go.

Ayebami *nods conspiratorially to* **Oyebisi**, *sits on the floor and brings out his divination tools. He performs a mock ritual until* **Awosika's Ghost** *possesses him.* **Ayebami** *copies the movements of* **Awosika's Ghost** *as he shakes the kola nuts and casts them.*

Ayebami   Ifa says the armies of your enemies outnumber your forces but they cannot defeat you unless the forest surrounding Oyo moves and it rains during harmattan. Awosika's amulets have made you invincible.

Oyebisi   Do you hear that, my lord?

Aderemi   This prophecy from Ifa raises my spirits. Can a forest move? Has it ever rained during the dry season?

Oyebisi   Never, my lord.

Awosika's Ghost *releases* **Ayebami** *from its spell.* **Ayebami**, *confused, looks for the source, following* **Awosika's Ghost**, *sensing it but not seeing it.* **Awosika's Ghost** *exits, with* **Ayebami** *following it.*

Aderemi Let them come. I will burn them with fire and trample their ashes underfoot. Neither their arrows nor their swords can pierce the hide of the Elephant. My wife! Olori[28] Oyebisi!

Oyebisi Yes, my king.

Aderemi We will press our enemies' necks to force them to attack before the harmattan winds blow over. Kundi!

Oyebisi Ashadele is an experienced general. How would you force such recklessness upon him?

Kundi *enters and bows.*

Kundi My lord.

Aderemi The houses of Ashadele, Opaleye and Iyan Agan still stand, do they not?

Kundi Yes, my lord?

Aderemi Is it wise to have my enemies in our midst?

Oyebisi The traitors are in exile, my lord.

Aderemi I am talking of their families who reap the benefits of their status while they plot against me.

Oyebisi My lord, they are women and children.

Aderemi You remember what you told me about my mentor Ogunwolu? How his men raped and pillaged your town.

Oyebisi The deaths of Iwalagba, Ogunwolu and Afilaka have sated my thirst for blood.

---

28 Queen.

Aderemi Should my own thirst not be sated?

Oyebisi But my lord, your thirst is that of a warrior's.

Aderemi You have spoken well. (*To* **Kundi**.) By the end of today, I want Ashadele, Opaleye and Iya Agan to hear that they are the last of their families.

Kundi *tarries.*

Oyebisi Please my lord, do not let it be said of me that the childless one has made her enemies childless.

Aderemi (*to* **Kundi**) Are you deaf? Go!

Kundi *exits.*

Oyebisi Worry not, my wife. I am the man you married.

Scene Fifteen

A few days later. Night. A courtyard in Ile-Ife.

Ashadele *with* **Opaleye**.

Ashadele When Ijaye heard that Ibadan had sent us a thousand men, they doubled their contribution to two thousand. The Borgu are sending their cavalry.

Opaleye Thank the gods, we have enough to overwhelm Oyo.

Ashadele We will use the harmattan haze as cover to get close to the city walls.

Opaleye The risk is our soldiers not recognising themselves and cutting each other down.

Ashadele The greater risk is being within sight of Aderemi's archers before we can breach the walls.

Opaleye Let us wait a few more weeks for the haze to clear. Put the Ekiti soldiers at the head of the advance.

Ashadele Basorun, I warned you not to take your dog with you to Ekiti, you didn't listen. They have joined cause with us, yet you still seek revenge?

Opaleye The only reason those dog-eaters are sending us soldiers is to weaken our grip on them. Wait and see how they will pillage the city before they return home. We have already lost Ilorin to the Fulani. The more of their soldiers we lose, the less of them we will face in the war to come. Whoever becomes Alaafin must rule over an empire that includes Ekiti.

Ashadele Speaking of which.

Ashadele *beckons to someone offstage.* **Adekanbi** *enters.* **Opaleye** *scowls at him.*

Ashadele Basorun, Aremo Adekanbi wishes to apologise for his past behaviour.

Ashadele *whacks* **Adekanbi** *over the head and points to the floor.* **Adekanbi** *glares at* **Ashadele**, *rubbing his head before making a half-hearted attempt at prostrating.*

Adekanbi (*mealy-mouthed*) Basorun, I am sorry.

Opaleye *sees he is not lying flat, hisses and looks away in disdain.*

Ashadele Adekanbi, apologise properly.

Adekanbi I am the crown prince.

Ashadele Do you want to become Alaafin?

Adekanbi *prostrates properly.*

Adekanbi Basorun Opaleye, I apologise for my behaviour. Please forgive me.

Ashadele (*pleads*) Basorun.

Opaleye I have been prime minister to your father, your grandfather and to the two kings before your royal house ascended the throne. Instead of seeking advice from me and preparing to follow in your father's footsteps, you roam all over the place, carrying women up and down. You are arrogant and irresponsible. You are too thick to learn. Why should the empire fall into your hands simply because of the blood that flows through your veins?

Adekanbi I am sorry, Basorun.

Opaleye If not that Aderemi has killed all the princes of the ruling houses, we would not even consider you as a candidate to succeed your father.

Adekanbi I know.

Opaleye You don't know anything! Brave men have shed blood because of you. Brave men will shed blood to put the crown on your useless head.

Ashadele He will understand in time.

Opaleye He needs to understand now. He is not a child. You beg only because you need us. But when you sit on the throne looking down on your subjects will you revert to your waywardness? In time, will they say, 'Life was better during the regency of Aderemi'? I cannot have it on my conscience that I installed a miscreant on the imperial throne. That cannot be my legacy. Think of the future, Aremo Adekanbi, son of Alaafin Iwalagba. Think of your legacy . . . Stand up.

As **Adekanbi** *stands,* **Iya Agan** *enters with the incredibly elderly but sprightly* **Moremi Ajasoro**. *She walks with an intricately carved walking stick. Her wrapper is made of aso oke.* **Ashadele** *and* **Opaleye** *drop to the floor in prostration.* **Ashadele** *drags* **Adekanbi** *back down to the floor.*

Opaleye Moremi Ajasoro, we prostrate before you.

Ashadele Moremi, saviour of our race.

Opaleye Our Mother Moremi.

Moremi Rise, my children.

They rise.

I hope you are being treated well.

Opaleye We have been treated like royalty, Our Mother.

Ashadele Ile-Ife has opened its arms to us.

Moremi Ashadele, I have a gift for you.

A **Servant** *enters with carvings of twins. He hands them to* **Ashadele**. **Ashadele** *wells up with emotion.*

Moremi Until you reunite with your twins.

Ashadele Thank you, Our Mother.

Moremi Have you heard from your families?

Opaleye Not since the last messenger from Oyo. But I am sure my wives are as quarrelsome as ever. My grandson will be spoiled rotten when next I see him.

Iya Agan He will not be as spoilt as my granddaughter.

Moremi (*chuckles*) A future husband and wife!

Opaleye If the gods will it, why not?

Iya Agan It has become increasingly difficult for them to escape the city.

Moremi The next news you hear of them will be the same as the last. No harm shall come to them.

Opaleye *Ase.*

Iya Agan I told Our Mother you were making battle plans.

Ashadele Our problem is how to breach the city walls without heavy casualties.

Moremi When the Bush People assaulted us with monsters . . .

Adekanbi We know the story.

They all give **Adekanbi** *withering looks.* **Adekanbi** *prostrates.*

Moremi When the Bush People assaulted us with monsters that struck fear into the hearts of our bravest warriors, that none of our charms could overcome, it was I Moremi Ajasoro who went as a spy into their midst and discovered their secret. The so-called monsters were soldiers disguised in raffia. I ran back to our land and revealed the secret. (*To* **Adekanbi**.) Remember how we defeated them?

Arms aching from prostrating, **Adekanbi** *does not realise she is talking to him.*

Moremi Wayward prince, I'm talking to you.

Adekanbi With fire, Our Mother.

Moremi Thank the *orisas*, there is something in that brain of yours.

Iya Agan The women are making raffia costumes for the first advance.

Opaleye Measure the Ekiti soldiers. They are leading the first wave.

Awosika's Ghost *appears.*

Ashadele Our Mother, everyone knows the story of Moremi Ajasoro. Aderemi and Oyebisi are not fools. Given that we are in harmattan and the foliage is dry, they only need to shoot a fiery arrow, and our soldiers will go up in flames as the Bush People did.

Opaleye In war there must be casualties.

Moremi Remember when Alaafin Sango made Timi of Ede fight Gbonka, the lord of magic and charms. Did Gbonka not extinguish Timi's fiery arrows?

Awosika's Ghost *whispers in* **Moremi Ajasoro**'s *ear. She reacts with alarm, then sorrow.*

Iya Agan We have consulted Ifa. The gods favour us.

Moremi Continue with your plans, Balogun. (*Sighs sadly.*) The battle is coming sooner than you would like.

Opaleye (*to* **Ashadele**) What did I tell you?

Iya Agan Our Mother, why this sudden sadness?

Moremi I need to rest.

Iya Agan *makes to go with her.*

Moremi Stay. The message is for the three of you and my lips cannot bear to relay it. The gods be with you and comfort you.

Iya Agan What message, Our Mother?

Moremi Ajasoro *exits with* **Awosika's Ghost**. **Aremo Adekanbi** *stands up, rubs his shoulders.*

Moremi (*off, wails*) Olu-Orogbo, oh!

Iya Agan Our Mother!

Opaleye She is calling for her son, Olu-Orogbo.

Adekanbi But he has been dead for ages.

Iya Agan It might portend bad news.

Ashadele I saw a dog crying. It looked like your late dog, Basorun.

Opaleye *Eewo!* Don't say that again.

A **Servant** *enters with a* **Messenger**.

Servant My lords, my lady. The messenger from Oyo.

The **Messenger** *kneels before them. The* **Servant** *exits.*

Opaleye You are welcome. What news from Oyo?

Messenger I did not wish to be the bearer of this news.

Ashadele Young man, you risked your life escaping Aderemi's spies. Now is not the time to be shy.

Messenger I wish it were shyness, my lord.

Adekanbi Spit it out and stop wasting our time!

Messenger Basorun Opaleye, Balogun Ashadele, Iya Agan. It pains me to say this, but you are now the last of your lineage.

Opaleye What did you say?

Iya Agan No . . .

Messenger Aderemi has put your families to the sword and laid waste to your compounds.

Ashadele He did not . . .

Iya Agan *falls to the ground wailing.* **Ashadele** *and* **Opaleye** *are stunned. The carvings drop from* **Ashadele***'s hands.*

Opaleye What did you say?

Messenger Please my lord, do not make me repeat myself.

Ashadele Even my newborn twins that he cradled in his arms?

Messenger I am so sorry, Balogun.

Opaleye My wife, my children. Gone, just like that?

Adekanbi (*without malice*) In war there are always casualties.

Opaleye *rushes at* **Adekanbi**. *The* **Messenger** *restrains* **Opaleye**.

Opaleye (*blind fury, stabbing his finger at* **Adekanbi**) You! You!

Adekanbi What did I say?

Ashadele Leave us.

Adekanbi *exits with the* **Messenger**. **Opaleye** *drops to the floor in tears.* **Ashadele** *stays standing but he is just as broken. He picks up the carvings and cradles them in his arms.*

Ashadele Sleep, my children. You are with your mother and your siblings.

The **Servant** *enters.* **Opaleye**, *despite his grief, stands up and stops crying, wiping the tears from his eyes.*

Opaleye Tell the generals to rally the troops. We march on Oyo tonight.

Ashadele *brings out* **Aderemi**'s *amulet and hold it up.*

Ashadele Aderemi, the gods curse me if you do not die by my sword!

Before the scene ends, **Oyebisi** *enters with a calabash. She puts gifts for the gods into the calabash one by one as an offering.*

Oyebisi The gods, please accept my offering. Cleanse me of my sin. Let Aderemi and me survive this war. *Ase.*

She closes the calabash and exits.

Scene Sixteen

The same day. Night. A sacred grove in which **Iyanifa** *sits.* **Esu** *inspects the offering and looks impressed. Around his neck is a necklace of red and black cowries.* **Iyanifa** *sniffs – there is a bad smell in the air.* **Oyebisi** *enters. She hesitates by the threshold.*

Iyanifa *Obinrin yi ma laya o.*[29]

Oyebisi *drops to her knees.*

Oyebisi Iyanifa, please.

Iyanifa You who reeks of my brother's blood, you dare to step foot in my shrine?

Oyebisi I have nowhere else to turn. The diviners all say they see nothing in my future. They say Esu rejects my sacrifices. They say, go to Iyanifa. Beg her to lift her curse.

---

29 The temerity of this woman.

Iyanifa And why would I do that? Why would I do anything for you except bring about your slow and painful death?

Oyebisi Iyanifa, yours is to relay what the gods have ordained.

Iyanifa Do not tell me my duty! I swear I will disavow my calling and rain curses on you!

Oyebisi Forgive me, Iyanifa.

Iyanifa How dare you? *How dare you*!

Oyebisi I'm sorry, Iyanifa.

Iyanifa 'Forgive me, I'm sorry'. Look at you. You fear the bloodlust you cultivated in Aderemi will consume you. That your enemies will take their revenge on you. You mocked Ifa and claimed your voice as Ifa's voice.

Oyebisi I did not foresee him killing babies. The twins . . .

Iyanifa You set all this in motion!

Oyebisi Oyo made me a slave. I wanted to reclaim my destiny.

Iyanifa At what price?

Oyebisi In my waking moments all I see are dead bodies of children floating in blood. My nightmares rage throughout the night. It is Awosika's doing. Please, beg him to forgive me. I did not mean to kill him.

Iyanifa Mention my brother's name again . . .

Esu *raises his hand to cut her off. He goes to* **Iyanifa** *with* **Oyebisi**'s *sacrifice. He puts the sacrifice down and hands* **Iyanifa** *his necklace to use instead of her usual necklace of white cowries. He whispers in her ear.* **Iyanifa** *looks at* **Esu**, *incredulous.* **Esu** *nods, encouraging* **Iyanifa** *to do his bidding.*

Iyanifa The witch cried in the night, the next morning the child died. Who does not know it is the witch that killed the child? Of course it is my brother that haunts you! You tainted him and then you killed him.

Oyebisi *bows her head to the ground.*

Oyebisi (*sobs*)   Forgive me, Iyanifa. Forgive me.

Iyanifa   Do not sully hallowed ground with your worthless tears!

Oyebisi *goes back up on her knees, wiping her eyes.* **Iyanifa** *casts the cowries.*

Iyanifa   Your wizard spoke the words of Ifa. The war will come to your doorstep. Aderemi shall sit on the throne and the crown placed on his head.

Oyebisi   What about me?

Iyanifa   That is all.

Oyebisi   Please . . .

Iyanifa   Be grateful that I have given you audience. Leave.

Oyebisi *exits.*

Iyanifa *turns to* **Esu**. **Esu**, *smiling, steps on the sacrifice, then pours blood over it.* **Iyanifa** *looks relieved.*

Iyanifa   Esu rejected your offering. Your destiny is in the hands of the god of the crossroads and he points his finger in three directions.

Scene Seventeen

Two weeks later. Split stage. The camps of Oyo and Ile-Ife. In the Oyo camp, we see men of fighting age fleeing the city. A sullen **Arokin** *beats a drum.*

Ayan   And so, both sides prepare for battle. Oyo rallies around their noble regent Aderemi and his wife Oyebisi. Archers from Ede arrive with their fiery arrows to man the city walls. Babies scarcely out of their mothers' wombs ask for swords and pledge their lives to defend Aderemi.

Kundi *enters, in battle garb.*

Kundi   Men are deserting in droves.

Aderemi   Execute the deserters.

Kundi *exits.*

Ayan   It was said that the enemies were so scared of Aderemi that anytime they heard his name they soiled themselves. The soldiers from Ibadan, Ijaye and Ekiti foresaw their deaths at the hand of the Elephant and fled back to their homes.

Oyebisi *enters.*

Aderemi   My wife. What word from Iyanifa?

Oyebisi   She says you will sit on the throne. The crown will be placed on your head.

Aderemi   The gods have always been on my side! Why do you look so sad?

In the Ile-Ife camp.

Servant (*announces*)   Seriki Ogedengbe, commander-in-chief of Ekiti's army.

Seriki Ogedengbe *enters. He greets* **Opaleye, Ashadele** *and* **Iya Agan** *warmly.*

Ashadele   Seriki Ogedengbe, you have brought twice the number of men!

Ogedengbe   We will sort out our differences after we have dealt with Aderemi. Please accept my condolences for your loss.

Ashadele   When the fighting starts, Aderemi is mine.

Opaleye   Brave Ashadele, if I were thirty years younger I would fight you for the right to face Aderemi. But we all know Awosika reinforced Aderemi's charms. Add the witchcraft of Ayebami and he is too strong even for you. Ogedengbe will slay him for us.

Ogedengbe Ashadele, I understand your desire for revenge, but it takes a warrior of legendary proportions to defeat a warrior as powerful as Aderemi. Why else would you seek my support?

Oyo camp.

Oyebisi My lord, executing more young men will demoralise the troops.

Aderemi They are of no consequence.

He holds up his charms.

Awosika's power is with me. No human being can kill me. If I must face the enemy's army alone, then face them alone I shall.

Oyebisi You are never alone, my husband.

Aderemi *hugs* **Oyebisi**. **Kundi** *eyes them.*

Ile-Ife camp.

Ashadele *shows* **Aderemi**'s *amulet to* **Ogedengbe**.

Ashadele Aderemi does not have a full set of amulets. Awosika's spirit will support me in ridding Oyo of him.

Ogedengbe And if he does not?

Ashadele Then he is yours to slay and I shall join my family.

Oyo camp.

Aderemi *puts on his necklace of amulets.* **Ayebami** *enters with an amulet to replace the missing amulet.*

Aderemi Now I am complete! Let my enemies come. I shall trample them underfoot!

A war drum sounds simultaneously in both camps.

Opaleye It is well. Now, let the hawk fly and tear out the eyes of the Elephant!

Aderemi/Ashadele To arms!

*The **Soldiers** on both sides raise a thunderous war chant.*

The soldiers of the Ile-Ife camp don their raffia costumes.

Scene Eighteen

The same day. The palace. In the background, the raffia-costumed army of Ile-Ife advance. **Aderemi**, **Oyebisi**, **Kundi** *and* **Ayebami**.

Aderemi My wife, Kundi will take you to safety.

Oyebisi I will stay within the palace walls.

Aderemi Just until after the battle is over.

Oyebisi I am where I should be, my lord.

Ayebami (*confidently*) And I too, my lord. Who has seen a tree walking? Who has seen a bush move by itself? Adele Aderemi, let us start calling you Kabiyesi!

Aderemi Soon, Ayebami.

*A **Soldier** dashes in.*

Soldier My lord, the forest is moving!

Oyebisi What?

Ayebami Impossible!

Ayebami *gets his charms ready.*

Aderemi Are you drunk?

Soldier No, my lord! The forest is moving like an army!

Oyebisi Like an army?

Soldier Yes, my lady!

Aderemi Tell the archers to light their arrows and train them on the forest.

Soldier Yes my lord!

The **Soldier** *exits.*

Aderemi Fools. They think we have forgotten the story of Moremi.

Esu *enters. The sound of rain.* **Esu** *dances in the rain.*

Aderemi I did not give the order for the cavalry to attack!

Oyebisi It's not the cavalry . . .

Thunder.

It's rain!

Ayebami *flees.*

Oyebisi Ifa lied to me!

Aderemi *draws his sword.*

Oyebisi Please, my lord, let us flee.

Aderemi The gods said the crown belongs to me!

Oyebisi The gods never spoke to us. Awosika spoke my words.

Aderemi What?

Oyebisi *falls to her knees.*

Oyebisi Please, my lord, we can escape before Ashadele's army surrounds the city.

Aderemi So, all this was done by my hand. All this and no intervention from the gods?

Oyebisi I am sorry, my lord. Please let us go.

Aderemi I, Aderemi, son of Ajasa the Blacksmith, wrestled with my destiny, with my self-doubt, with spiritual forces and I won.

Oyebisi Please, my lord.

Aderemi Don't you see? There is only this final obstacle in my way. I still have Awosika's charms. Let them come with their arrows and swords and die trying to pierce the Elephant's hide.

Oyebisi: Please, my love!

Aderemi (*holds her face in his hand*) You are my *orisa*. You made this happen. After I finish with our enemies, you shall place the crown on my head, and we shall rule over the empire. It started with your dream and it shall end with your dream coming true. Kundi!

Kundi My lord!

Aderemi Protect your mistress with your life.

Kundi *draws his sword.* **Aderemi** *exits.* **Oyebisi** *watches him leave.*

In the background, **Aderemi** *scythes down the enemy. At first, the* **Oyo** *army has the upper hand.* **Ashadele** *and* **Ogedengbe** *enter the fray and force the* **Oyo** *army into a retreat.*

Oyo Soldiers Retreat! Retreat to the palace!

Oyebisi *recoils as two* **Ile-Ife Soldiers** *dressed in raffia outfits enter.*

Kundi We must leave, my lady!

Oyebisi My husband . . .

Kundi *grabs her by the arm and runs away with her, chased by the* **Ile-Ife Soldiers**. *The* **Oyo Soldiers** *dash into the palace. They try to fight off the chasing* **Ile-Ife Soldiers**. *They drop their weapons and flee, chased by the* **Ile-Ife Soldiers**. *Offstage we hear their screams as they are killed.* **Aderemi** *enters, his arms soaked in* *enemy blood. The two* **Ile-Ife Soldiers** *enter. They attack* **Aderemi**. *He kills them easily.* **Ogedengbe** *enters.*

Ogedengbe Aderemi! *Iku ba e l'eni.*[30]

Aderemi Ogedengbe! Today I shall cut off your head. This time let's see if you will pick it up and place it back on your traitorous neck.

As they are about to engage. **Ashadele** *enters.*

Ashadele He is mine!

Ogedengbe, *thirsty for* **Aderemi**'s *blood, relents.*

Ashadele By the gods, the blood of my twins will be avenged.

Aderemi You call on the gods as if you have never spilled innocent blood.

Ashadele Not today.

Aderemi Today, yesterday, is it not the same innocent blood that fuels our ambition? If I must pay, so must you!

Ashadele Killer of babies, this is where your reign of terror ends!

Awosika's Ghost *appears.*

Aderemi Because the Hawk flies, it thinks it can subdue the Elephant. Awosika's charms have made me impenetrable to weapons or charms.

Awosika's Ghost *'takes' the power of* **Aderemi**'s *charms and transfers it to* **Ashadele**. **Opaleye** *and* **Iya Agan** *enter.* **Ashadele** *holds up* **Aderemi**'s *charm.*

Ashadele Then in my hand I hold the spear that will pierce your hide. I took this from the hand of Iwalagba whom you murdered.

Aderemi It is one amulet out of many.

---

30 You will meet your end today.

Ashadele It shall be enough to kill you.

They fight. **Aderemi** *is superior to* **Ashadele** *and has the upper hand, cutting* **Ashadele** *a few times.* **Ogedengbe** *makes to assist* **Ashadele**. **Opaleye** *stops him.* **Ogedengbe** *looks to* **Iya Agan** *for support but she sides with* **Opaleye**.

Awosika *guides* **Ashadele**'s *sword arm, feinting and parrying* **Aderemi**'s *strikes and then guiding* **Ashadele** *to cut* **Aderemi**. **Aderemi** *looks in shock.*

Ashadele So, the Elephant's hide can be pierced.

Iya Agan Aderemi, the gods have deserted you. Surrender and face justice.

Aderemi *takes off his charm, throws it away and attacks* **Ashadele**. *They fight furiously until* **Ashadele** *stabs* **Aderemi**. **Aderemi** *drops his sword and crawls to the throne. He dies at the foot of the throne.*

Iya Agan It is done.

Ashadele Oyebisi still breathes.

Ogedengbe If our men find her, how should they bring her to you: dead or alive?

Ashadele, **Iya Agan** *and* **Opaleye** *give him a dirty look. He understands.*

Awosika's Ghost, *avenged, disappears.*

A **Soldier** *enters.*

Soldier The Oyo soldiers have surrendered! We have taken them prisoner.

Arokin *enters. He is still in* **Ayan**'s *clothes.*

Iya Agan Arokin!

Arokin I am glad to see you all alive.

Ashadele We too are glad you survived this tyrant's brief but brutal reign.

Iya Agan Why are you dressed in Ayan's clothes?

Arokin My reward for telling the truth.

Opaleye As soon as Oyebisi's corpse lies next to her husband, we must bury this episode of our history. That we let a man like Aderemi to get this far to the throne is a stain on all of us. See how many we are, and we let one man brutalise us and bend us to his will. It must never happen again.

All *Ase.*

Arokin I'm afraid I must record events as they occurred otherwise future generations will make the same mistake. I cannot leave anything out.

Ashadele I agree. Arokin, you must tell the truth.

Iya Agan Leave nothing out.

Opaleye It is well. Now to tell Adekanbi to prepare his head for the crown.

Iya Agan Is it not possible that he died during the battle?

Ashadele Iya Agan, he is miles away in Ile-Ife.

Iya Agan I hear the Ede archers have an excellent aim.

Ashadele He will reign dutifully. We will make sure of it.

Iya Agan Only the gods can make that a certainty.

Ashadele We must not abdicate our duty to the gods. We have lost too much not to realise that simple fact.

Opaleye Come, let us return to our camp. We must thank our ancestors and deities who fought on our behalf and made the Oyo Empire whole again.

Ogedengbe Go on ahead.

They exit. **Ogedengbe** *makes sure they are out of earshot.*

Ogedengbe You are an Ekiti soldier, are you not?

Soldier Yes, my lord.

Ogedengbe Kill the prisoners.

The **Soldier** *looks in surprise at* **Ogedengbe**, *then smiles.*

Soldier Yes, my lord.

Soldier *exits.*

Ogedengbe *exits.*

Two figures dressed in the raffia outfit enter. One of them holds the Alaafin's crown and looks over **Aderemi**'s *body while the other stays vigilant. They remove the head dress of their outfits to reveal it is* **Oyebisi** *holding the crown and* **Kundi**. **Oyebisi** *looks tearfully at* **Aderemi**'s *body.*

Kundi My lady we must leave before the soldiers return.

Oyebisi Leave us.

Kundi My lady . . .

Oyebisi Go.

Kundi *reluctantly exits.* **Oyebisi** *drags* **Aderemi**'s *body, trying to put it on the throne but he is too heavy for her. She grabs the crown and puts it on his head.*

Oyebisi Kabiyesi.

Oyebisi *cradles* **Aderemi**'s *head.*

Arokin, *restored to his status and robes enters, followed by a penitent* **Ayan** *back in his role and clothes as praise-singer.*

Arokin (*to* **Ayan**) I'm not a petty man, Ayan. I swear, all is forgiven.

Ayan *prostrates before* **Arokin**.

Ayan Thank you, Arokin. The gods bless you.

Ayan *stands up and drums softly, accompanying* **Arokin**.

Arokin What happened to Oyebisi? Some say she was captured and executed. Others say she was captured but sold into slavery. Others say she escaped and lived to a ripe old age while others say she disappeared into the harmattan mist never to be seen or heard of again.

Two **Soldiers** *enter.* **Arokin** *nods to* **Ayan**. *They grab him.*

Ayan Please! Arokin! Arokin!

Arokin Others say she married Kundi, that they conquered and reigned over a hinterland village while others say she met and married a king and founded a dynasty. Still others say she was chased into a river and returned as a goddess that is worshipped until today. While others say she died and was reincarnated into (*points to an audience member*) you. (*To another audience member.*) Or you. (*To another.*) Or you. For now, in the words of Basorun Opaleye, it is well!

The End.

Discover. Read. Listen. Watch.

A NEW WAY TO ENGAGE WITH PLAYS

This award-winning digital library features over 3,000 playtexts, 400 audio plays, 300 hours of video and 360 scholarly books.

Playtexts published by Methuen Drama, The Arden Shakespeare, Faber & Faber, Playwrights Canada Press, Aurora Metro Books and Nick Hern Books.

Audio Plays from L.A. Theatre Works featuring classic and modern works from the oeuvres of leading American playwrights.

Video collections including films of live performances from the RSC, The Globe and The National Theatre, as well as acting masterclasses and BBC feature films and documentaries.

FIND OUT MORE:
www.dramaonlinelibrary.com • @dramaonlinelib

Methuen Drama Modern Plays

include

Bola Agbaje
Ayad Akhtar
Edward Albee
Jean Anouilh
John Arden
Peter Barnes
Clare Barron
Sebastian Barry
Alistair Beaton
Brendan Behan
Edward Bond
William Boyd
Bertolt Brecht
Howard Brenton
Amelia Bullmore
Anthony Burgess
Leo Butler
Jim Cartwright
Lolita Chakrabarti
Caryl Churchill
Lucinda Coxon
Tim Crouch
Shelagh Delaney
Ishy Din
Claire Dowie
David Edgar
David Eldridge
Dario Fo
Michael Frayn
John Godber
James Graham
David Greig
John Guare
Lauren Gunderson
Peter Handke
David Harrower
Jonathan Harvey
Robert Holman
David Ireland
Sarah Kane

Barrie Keeffe
Jasmine Lee-Jones
Anders Lustgarten
Duncan Macmillan
David Mamet
Patrick Marber
Martin McDonagh
Alistair McDowall
Arthur Miller
Tom Murphy
Phyllis Nagy
Anthony Neilson
Peter Nichols
Ben Okri
Joe Orton
Vinay Patel
Joe Penhall
Luigi Pirandello
Stephen Poliakoff
Lucy Prebble
Peter Quilter
Mark Ravenhill
Philip Ridley
Willy Russell
Sam Shepard
Martin Sherman
Chris Shinn
Jackie Sibblies Drury
Wole Soyinka
Simon Stephens
Kae Tempest
Laura Wade
Anne Washburn
Timberlake Wertenbaker
Roy Williams
Snoo Wilson
Theatre Workshop
Frances Ya-Chu Cowhig
Benjamin Zephaniah

Methuen Drama Student Editions

Alan Ayckbourn *Confusions* • **Mike Bartlett** *Earthquakes in London* • **Aphra Behn** *The Rover* • **Alice Birch** *Revolt. She Said. Revolt Again* • **Edward Bond** *Lear* • *Saved* • **Bertolt Brecht** *The Caucasian Chalk Circle* • *Fear and Misery in the Third Reich* • *The Good Person of Szechwan* • *Life of Galileo* • *Mother Courage and her Children* • *The Resistible Rise of Arturo Ui* • *The Threepenny Opera* • **Jon Brittain** *Rotterdam* • **Georg Büchner** *Woyzeck* • **Anton Chekhov** *The Cherry Orchard* • *The Seagull* • *Three Sisters* • *Uncle Vanya* • **Caryl Churchill** *Serious Money* • *Top Girls* • **Shelagh Delaney** *A Taste of Honey* • **Inua Ellams** *Barber Shop Chronicles* • **Euripides** *Elektra* • *Medea* • **Dario Fo** *Accidental Death of an Anarchist* • **Michael Frayn** *Copenhagen* • **John Galsworthy** *Strife* • **Nikolai Gogol** *The Government Inspector* • **Carlo Goldoni** *A Servant to Two Masters* • **James Graham** *This House* • **Tanika Gupta** *The Empress* • **Katori Hall** *The Mountaintop* • **Lorraine Hansberry** *A Raisin in the Sun* • **Robert Holman** *Across Oka* • **Henrik Ibsen** *A Doll's House* • *Ghosts* • *Hedda Gabler* • **Sarah Kane** *4.48 Psychosis* • *Blasted* • **Charlotte Keatley** *My Mother Said I Never Should* • **Dennis Kelly** *DNA* • **Bernard Kops** *Dreams of Anne Frank* • **Federico García Lorca** *Blood Wedding* • *Doña Rosita the Spinster* (bilingual edition) • *The House of Bernarda Alba* (bilingual edition) • *Yerma* (bilingual edition) • **David Mamet** *Glengarry Glen Ross* • *Oleanna* • **Patrick Marber** *Closer* • **John Marston** *The Malcontent* • **Martin McDonagh** *The Lieutenant of Inishmore* • *The Lonesome West* • *The Beauty Queen of Leenane* • *The Cripple of Inishmaan* • **Alistair McDowall** *Pomona* • **John McGrath** *The Cheviot, the Stag and the Black, Black Oil* • **Arthur Miller** *All My Sons* • *The Crucible* • *A View from the Bridge* • *Death of a Salesman* • *The Price* • *After the Fall* • *The Last Yankee* • *A Memory of Two Mondays* • *Broken Glass* • *Incident at Vichy* • *The American Clock* • *The Ride Down Mt. Morgan* • **Joe Orton** *Loot* • **Joe Penhall** *Blue/Orange* • **Luigi Pirandello** *Six Characters in Search of an Author* • **Lucy Prebble** *Enron* • **Mark Ravenhill** *Shopping and F***ing* • **Reginald Rose** *Twelve Angry Men* • **Willy Russell** *Blood Brothers* • *Educating Rita* • **Lemn Sissay** Benjamin Zephaniah's *Refugee Boy* • **Sophocles** *Antigone* • *Oedipus the King* • **Wole Soyinka** *Death and the King's Horseman* • **Simon Stephens** *Punk Rock* • *Pornography* • **Shelagh Stephenson** *The Memory of Water* • **August Strindberg** *Miss Julie* • **J. M. Synge** *The Playboy of the Western World* • **Kae Tempest** *Wasted* • **Theatre Workshop** *Oh What a Lovely War* • **Laura Wade** *Posh* • **Frank Wedekind** *Spring Awakening* • **Timberlake Wertenbaker** *Our Country's Good* • **Arnold Wesker** *The Merchant* • **Peter Whelan** *The Accrington Pals* • **Oscar Wilde** *The Importance of Being Earnest* • **Roy Williams** *Sing Yer Heart Out for the Lads* • **Tennessee Williams** *A Streetcar Named Desire* • *The Glass Menagerie* • *Cat on a Hot Tin Roof* • *Sweet Bird of Youth*

Methuen Drama Contemporary Dramatists
include

John Arden (two volumes)
Arden & D'Arcy
Peter Barnes (three volumes)
Sebastian Barry
Mike Bartlett
Clare Barron
Brad Birch
Dermot Bolger
Edward Bond (ten volumes)
Howard Brenton (two volumes)
Leo Butler (two volumes)
Richard Cameron
Jim Cartwright
Caryl Churchill (two volumes)
Complicite
Sarah Daniels (two volumes)
Nick Darke
David Edgar (three volumes)
David Eldridge (two volumes)
Ben Elton
Per Olov Enquist
Dario Fo (two volumes)
Michael Frayn (four volumes)
John Godber (four volumes)
Paul Godfrey
James Graham (two volumes)
David Greig
John Guare
Lee Hall (two volumes)
Katori Hall
Peter Handke
Jonathan Harvey (two volumes)
Iain Heggie
Israel Horovitz
Declan Hughes
Terry Johnson (three volumes)
Sarah Kane
Barrie Keeffe
Bernard-Marie Koltès (two volumes)
Franz Xaver Kroetz
Kwame Kwei-Armah
David Lan
Bryony Lavery
Deborah Levy
Doug Lucie
Alistair MacDowall
Sabrina Mahfouz
David Mamet (six volumes)
Patrick Marber
Martin McDonagh
Duncan McLean
David Mercer (two volumes)
Anthony Minghella (two volumes)
Rory Mullarkey
Tom Murphy (six volumes)
Phyllis Nagy
Anthony Neilson (three volumes)
Peter Nichol (two volumes)
Philip Osment
Gary Owen
Louise Page
Stewart Parker (two volumes)
Joe Penhall (two volumes)
Stephen Poliakoff (three volumes)
David Rabe (two volumes)
Mark Ravenhill (three volumes)
Christina Reid
Philip Ridley (two volumes)
Willy Russell
Eric-Emmanuel Schmitt
Ntozake Shange
Sam Shepard (two volumes)
Martin Sherman (two volumes)
Christopher Shinn (two volumes)
Joshua Sobel
Wole Soyinka (two volumes)
Simon Stephens (five volumes)
Shelagh Stephenson
David Storey (three volumes)
C. P. Taylor
Sue Townsend
Judy Upton (two volumes)
Michel Vinaver (two volumes)
Arnold Wesker (two volumes)
Peter Whelan
Michael Wilcox
Roy Williams (four volumes)
David Williamson
Snoo Wilson (two volumes)
David Wood (two volumes)
Victoria Wood

For a complete listing of
Methuen Drama titles, visit:
www.bloomsbury.com/drama

Follow us on X and keep up to date with
our news and publications
@MethuenDrama